Hans Küng, who was born in  the Gregorian University in a Roman Catholic priest in 1. of Tübingen (1960–96), where he also ance for Ecumenical Research from 1963. In 1962 he was named by Pope John XXIII a peritus (theological consultant) for the Second Vatican Council. He played a central role in the writing of Vatican II, which from 1962 to 1965 radically modernised key areas of Catholic teaching and practice. He has since the early 1960s questioned traditional church doctrines such as papal infallibility. In 1979 a Vatican censure that banned his teaching as a Catholic theologian provoked huge international controversy but the University appointed him to a personal chair of ecumenical theology. On his retirement in 1996 he became President of the Global Ethic Foundation in Tübingen. He remains a Catholic priest in good standing. His many books include *On Being a Christian* (1974), *Does God Exist?* (1978), *Global Responsibility* (1991) and *Christianity: Its Essence and History* (1994).

By Hans Küng

On Being a Christian
Does God Exist?
Global Responsibility
Christianity: Its Essence and History
The Catholic Church

Other titles in the Phoenix Press
Universal History series

The Renaissance *Paul Johnson*
The Balkans *Mark Mazower*
Islam *Karen Armstrong*
Communism *Richard Pipes*
The German Empire 1871–1919 *Michael Stürmer*
Peoples and Empires *Anthony Pagden*
Hitler and the Holocaust *Robert Wistrich*

THE CATHOLIC CHURCH

Hans Küng

Translated by John Bowden

PHOENIX
PRESS

5 UPPER SAINT MARTIN'S LANE
LONDON
WC2H 9EA

To
Dr John Bowden
in gratitude

A PHOENIX PRESS PAPERBACK

First published in Great Britain in 2001
by Weidenfeld & Nicolson
This paperback edition published in 2002
by Phoenix Press,
an imprint of Orion Books Ltd,
Orion House, 5 Upper St Martin's Lane,
London WC2H 9EA

Third impression 2002

A CIP catalogue record for this book
is available from the British Library.

ISBN 1 84212 494 3

Printed and bound in Great Britain by
Clays Ltd, St Ives plc

Contents

Introduction: The Catholic Church in Conflict

As the author of *The Catholic Church: A Short History* I want to say quite openly, right at the beginning, that despite all my experiences of how merciless the Roman system can be, the Catholic Church, this fellowship of believers, has remained my spiritual home to the present day.

That has consequences for this book. Of course the history of the Catholic Church can also be told in a different way. A 'neutral' description of it can be given by experts in religion or historians who are not personally involved in this history. Or it can be described by a 'hermeneutical' philosopher or theologian, concerned with 'understanding', for whom to understand everything is also to forgive everything. However, I have written this history as someone who is involved in it. I can 'understand' phenomena like intellectual repression and the Inquisition, the burning of witches, the persecution of Jews and discrimination against women from the historical context, but that does not mean that I can therefore 'forgive' them in any way. I write as one who takes the side of those who became victims, or already in their time recognized and censured particular church practices as being unchristian.

To be quite specific and quite personal, I write as one who was born into a Catholic family, in the little Swiss Catholic town of Sursee, and who went to school in the Catholic city of Lucerne. I then lived for seven whole years in Rome in the elite papal Collegium Germanicum et Hungaricum and studied philosophy and theology at the pontifical Gregorian University. When I was ordained priest I celebrated the eucharist for the first time in St Peter's and gave my first sermon to a congregation of Swiss Guards.

After gaining my doctorate in theology at the Institut Catholique in Paris I worked for two years as a pastor in Lucerne. Then in 1960, at the age of thirty-two, I became Professor of Catholic Theology at the University of Tübingen.

I took part in the Second Vatican Council between 1962 and 1965 as an expert nominated by John XXIII, taught in Tübingen for two decades, and founded the Institute for Ecumenical Research, of which I was director.

In 1979 I then had personal experience of the Inquisition under another pope. My permission to teach was withdrawn by the church, but nevertheless I retained my chair and my Institute (which was separated from the Catholic Faculty as a result).

For two further decades I remained unswervingly faithful to my church in critical loyalty and to the present day I have remained Professor of Ecumenical Theology and a Catholic priest 'in good standing'.

I affirm the papacy for the Catholic Church, but at the same time indefatigably call for a radical reform of it in accordance with the criterion of the gospel.

With a history and a Catholic past like this, should I not be capable of writing a history of the Catholic Church which is both committed and objective? Perhaps it could prove even more exciting to hear the story of this church from an insider who has been involved in such a way. Of course I shall be just as concerned to be objective as any 'neutral' (if there really are such people in matters of religion). However, I am convinced that personal commitment and matter-of-fact objectivity can as well be combined in a history of the church as they can in the history of a nation.

I venture to offer this short history of the church, then, as someone who has much experience in church affairs and has been much tested by them. Of course it cannot replace the large multi-volume works – those edited by A. Fliche and V. Martin; by H. Jedin; by L. J. Rogier, R. Aubert and M. D. Knowles; or by M. Mollart du Jourdin – of which I have made use, nor is it meant to. But since I have both studied this history all my life and lived out some of it, my book is quite distinctive.

I have already grappled with the history of the Catholic Church in my earlier books, *The Council and Reunion* (1960, English translation 1961), *Structures of the Church* (1962, Eng. trans. 1965), and *The Church* (1967, Eng. trans. 1971); and I continued to do so later, in *On Being a Christian* (1974, Eng. trans. 1977), *Does God Exist? An Answer for Today* (1978, Eng. trans. 1980), *Theology for the Third Millennium: An Ecumenical View* (1984, Eng. trans. 1988), *Judaism* (1991, Eng. trans. 1992) and *Great Christian Thinkers* (1993, Eng. trans. 1994). I gave an analytical synthesis of the whole history of Christianity in my *Christianity: Its Essence and History* (1994, Eng. trans. 1995). In this book I described its various epoch-making paradigms, not only the Roman Catholic paradigm but also the original Jewish-Christian paradigm, the Hellenistic-Byzantine Slavonic paradigm, the paradigm of the Protestant Reformation and the paradigm of the Enlightenment and modernity. Here the reader will find a wealth of bibliographical references for the history of the Roman Catholic Church and, of course, also many ideas and perspectives which I shall take up in a new way in this short book. I shall do so briefly, and I shall concentrate on the main lines, structures and figures, without making use of scholarly ballast (there are no notes and no bibliographical references).

As I write, I am keenly aware that views about this Catholic Church and its history diverge widely, both inside and outside the church. Probably more than any other church, the Catholic Church is a controversial church, subject to extremes of admiration and attack.

Beyond question the history of the Catholic Church is a history of success: the Catholic Church is the oldest, numerically the strongest, and probably also the most powerful representative of Christianity. There is great admiration for the vitality of this two-thousand-year-old church; its organization, which was global before any talk of 'globalization' and at the same time effective locally; its strict hierarchy and the solidity of its dogmas; its worship, rich in tradition and colourful in its splendour; its indisputable cultural achievements in building up and shaping the West. Optimistic and idealistic church historians and theologians think that they can discern an organic growth in this history, in doctrine, constitution, law, liturgy and piety. They claim that the Catholic Church is like a gigantic old tree, which while continuing to bear rotting fruit and to put forth dead branches, can still be understood to be in a process of permanent development, unfolding and becoming perfect. Here the history of the Catholic Church is understood as an organic process of maturing and spreading.

But even traditional Catholics are now asking: Supposing that there is organic growth, are there not also within the history of the Catholic Church quite unorganic, abnormal, completely nonsensical false developments, for which the church's official representatives are themselves responsible? Despite all the grandiose talk of progress, are there not also terrifying lapses, for which the popes are anything but blameless?

During the time of the Second Vatican Council (1962–5) the Catholic Church enjoyed a generally high public standing. At the beginning of the third millennium after Christ, however, it is being attacked more than ever in some quarters. Granted, Rome has recently been asking 'for forgiveness' for the monstrous errors and atrocities of the past – but in the meantime, the present-day church administration and inquisition are producing still more victims. Scarcely any of the great institutions in our democratic age deals in such a despicable way with critics and those of other views in its own ranks, nor does any discriminate so much against women – by prohibiting contraceptives, the marriage of priests and the ordination of women. None polarizes society and politics worldwide to such a degree by rigid positions in matters of abortion, homosexuality and euthanasia – positions always invested with an aura of infallibility, as if they were the will of God himself.

In view of the apparent inability on the part of the Catholic Church to correct and reform itself, is it not understandable that at the beginning of the third Christian millennium the more or less benevolent indifference widely shown to the church around fifty years ago has turned into hatred, indeed public hostility? Antagonistic church historians and critics are of the opinion that in the church's two-thousand-year history no organic process of maturing can be detected, but rather something more like a 'criminal history'. A once-Catholic author, Karlheinz Deschner, has devoted his life, and so far six volumes, to such a history. In it he describes every possible form of 'criminality' in the church's foreign policy and policies relating to trade, finance and education; in the dissemination of ignorance and superstition; in the unscrupulous exploitation of sexual morality, marriage laws and penal justice ... And so on, for hundreds of pages.

So while some Catholic theologians are busy writing church history in a triumphalist vein, anti-Catholic 'criminologists' eager for scandal are exploiting it in order to put down the Catholic Church by any means possible. But by similarly summarizing and amassing all the errors, wrong turns and crimes that can be discovered anywhere, would it not also be possible to write a 'criminal' history of Germany, France, England or the USA – not to mention the monstrous crimes of modern atheists in the name of the goddess reason or nation, race or party? And does such a fixation on the negative side do justice to the history of Germany, France, England or America – or the Catholic Church? I am presumably not the only one who finds that, over time, such a multi-volume *Criminal History of Christianity* becomes insipid, unexciting, boring. Those who deliberately step in all the puddles should not complain too loudly about how bad the road is.

Neither an idealizing and romanticized history of the church nor one filled with hatred and denunciation can be taken seriously. Something else is called for.

Like the history of other institutions, the history of the Catholic Church, too, is a chequered one. The Catholic Church is a vast, efficient organization, employing an apparatus of power and finance operating with highly worldly means. Behind the imposing statistics, the great occasions and the solemn liturgies of Catholic masses there is all too frequently a superficial traditional Christianity with little substance. In the disciplined Catholic hierarchy it is often depressingly evident that there is a body of functionaries, constantly with an eye on Rome, servile

towards superiors and arrogant towards inferiors. The closed
dogmatic system of teaching comprises a long outdated authoritarian and unbiblical scholastic theology. And the Catholic
Church's highly praised contribution to Western culture is inex-
tricably bound up with a worldly nature and a deviation from
its own spiritual tasks.

However, despite everything, such categories do not do full
justice to the life of this church as it is lived, to its spirit. The
Catholic Church has remained a spiritual power, indeed a great
power, all over the world, which neither Nazism, Stalinism nor
Maoism has been able to destroy. Moreover, quite apart from
its great organization, on all fronts in this world it has at its
disposal a uniquely broad base of communities, hospitals,
schools and social institutions in which an infinite amount of
good is done, despite all their weaknesses. Here many pastors
wear themselves out in the service of their fellow men and
women, and countless women and men devote themselves to
young and old, the poor, the sick, the disadvantaged and the
failures. Here is a worldwide community of believers and committed people.

If we are to differentiate good from evil within the church's
ambiguous history and ambiguous present circumstances, we
need a fundamental criterion to judge by. In a work of church
history, no matter what scholarly 'neutrality' over values may
be claimed, time and again facts, developments, persons and
institutions are tacitly subjected to an evaluation. This history
is no different.

I am convinced that any theology and any council – however
much it is to be understood in terms of its time and the time
preceding it – must, insofar as it claims to be Christian, ultimately be judged by the criterion of what is Christian. And the

criterion of what is Christian – also according to the view of the councils and the popes – is the original Christian message, the gospel, indeed the original figure of Christianity: the concrete, historical Jesus of Nazareth, who for Christians is the Messiah, that Jesus Christ from whom any Christian church derives its existence. And of course this point of view has consequences for any account of the history of the Catholic Church. At any rate it does for mine.

A distinguishing mark of my history will be the way in which tacitly, and indeed at crucial junctures explicitly and without compromise and harmonization, it will face up to the original Christian message, the gospel, indeed to Jesus Christ himself. Without such a reference, a Christian church would have neither identity nor relevance. All Catholic institutions, dogmas, legal rulings and ceremonies are subject to the criterion whether, in this sense, they are 'Christian' or at least not 'anti-Christian': whether they accord with the gospel. That is also made clear from the fact that this book by a Catholic theologian about the Catholic Church at the same time seeks to be evangelical, that is to say subject to the norm of the gospel. It thus seeks to be both 'Catholic' and 'evangelical' at the same time, indeed ecumenical in the deepest sense of the word.

In our information age the media expose us to a steadily growing flood of information about the history of Christianity and Christianity today, and the Internet increasingly offers not only valuable information but also mountains of useless material. Thus knowledgeable selection is called for to distinguish the important from the unimportant. Although this short history of the Catholic Church seeks to convey facts, above all it is intended to provide orientation in three respects.

- First, basic information about the tremendously dramatic and complex historical development of the Catholic Church: not about all the countless currents and the leading personalities of different eras or territories, but about the main lines of development, dominant structures and influential figures.

- Secondly, a critical historical stocktaking of twenty centuries of the Catholic Church. Of course there will be no petty condemnation and quibbling, but for all the chronological narrative, time and again there will be objective analysis and criticism to indicate how and why the Catholic Church has become what it is today.

- Thirdly, a concrete challenge to introduce reform in the direction of what the Catholic Church is, and could be. There will certainly not be extrapolations and prognoses of the future, which no one can give, but there will be realistic perspectives offering hope for a church which, I am convinced, still has a future in the third millennium – provided that it fundamentally renews itself, in keeping both with the gospel and the age.

So, at the end of this introduction, a warning is in order to readers (especially Catholic readers) who are relatively uninformed about history. Those who so far have not been seriously confronted with the facts of history will sometimes be shocked at how human the course of events was everywhere; indeed, how many of the institutions and constitutions of the church – and especially the central Roman Catholic institution of the papacy – are man-made. However, this very fact means that these institutions and constitutions – including the papacy in particular – can be changed and reformed. My critical 'destruction' is offered in the service of 'construction', reform and renewal, so that the Catholic Church remains capable of life in the third millennium.

For in spite of all the radical criticism of the church, it has probably already become clear that I am buoyed up by an unshakeable faith. This is not faith in the church as an institution, since quite obviously the church continually fails, but faith in Jesus Christ, his person and cause, which remains the prime motif in the church's tradition, liturgy and theology. For all the decadence of the church, Jesus Christ has never been lost. The name of Jesus Christ is something like the 'golden thread' in the tapestry of church history. Though often the tapestry is torn and grubby, that thread is constantly worked in again.

Only the spirit of this Jesus Christ can give the Catholic Church, and Christianity generally, a new credibility and enable it to be understood. But precisely when one reflects on the origins of Christianity, its starting point, a fundamental question arises which cannot be passed over in a church history. Did Jesus of Nazareth found a church at all?

I   *The Beginnings of the Church*

Founded by Jesus?

According to the Gospels, the man from Nazareth virtually never used the word 'church'. There are no sayings of Jesus spoken in public which programmatically call for a community of the elect and for the founding of a church. Biblical critics are agreed on this point: Jesus did not proclaim a church, nor did he proclaim himself, but the kingdom of God. Governed by the awareness of living in an end time, Jesus wanted to announce God's imminent kingdom, God's rule, with a view to human salvation. He did not call simply for the external observance of God's commandments, but for their fulfilment in commitment to one's neighbour. In short, Jesus called for a benevolent love which includes even one's opponent, indeed one's enemy. Love of God and love of neighbour are called for to the same degree as love of oneself ('Love ... as yourself'), as they are already in the Hebrew Bible.

Thus Jesus, a powerful preacher of the Word and at the same time a charismatic healer of the body and the soul, called together a great eschatological collective movement, and for him the Twelve with Peter were a sign of the restoration of the full number of the tribes of Israel. To the annoyance of the pious and the orthodox he also invited into this kingdom those of other religious beliefs (Samaritans), those who were politically compromised (tax collectors), those who had failed morally (adulterers), and those who were exploited sexually (prostitutes). For him, specific precepts of the law, above all those relating to food, cleanness and the sabbath, were secondary to love of neighbour; the sabbath and the commandments are there for men and women.

Jesus was a provocative prophet, who showed that he was critical of the temple, and indeed engaged in a militant demonstration against the commerce which was so prominent there. Although he was not a political revolutionary, his words and actions thus soon brought him into a fatal conflict with the political and religious establishment. Indeed, in the view of many this young man of thirty, with no specific office or title, transcended the claim of a mere rabbi or prophet, so that they saw him as the Messiah.

However, in his amazingly brief activity – at most three years or perhaps only a few months – he did not seek to found a separate community distinct from Israel with its own creed and cult, or to call to life an organization with its own constitution and offices, let alone a great religious edifice. No, according to all the evidence, Jesus did not found a church in his lifetime.

But we must now immediately add that a church in the sense of a religious community distinct from Israel came into being immediately after Jesus's death. This happened under the impact of the experience of the resurrection and the Spirit. It was reported that on the basis of particular charismatic experiences ('appearances', visions, auditions) and a particular pattern in the interpretation of the Hebrew Bible (persecuted prophet, suffering servant of God), the Jewish followers of Jesus, men and women, became convinced that this man whom they themselves betrayed, this man who was mocked and scorned by his opponents, this man who was forsaken by God and his fellow human beings and perished on the cross with a loud cry, did not remain dead. They believed that he had been raised by God to eternal life, and had been exalted into God's glory, fully in keeping with the image in Psalm 110, 'he sits at the right hand of God', made by God 'Lord and Messiah' (cf. Acts 2.22–36), 'appointed Son of God in power on the basis of the resurrection from the dead' (Romans 1.3f.).

So this is the answer to the question. Although the church was not founded by Jesus, for its origins it made an appeal to him: the one who was crucified yet lived, in whom for believers the kingdom of God had already dawned. It remained the Jesus movement with an eschatological orientation; its basis was initially not its own cult, its own constitution, its own organization with specific offices. Its foundation was simply the confession in faith of this Jesus as the Messiah, the Christ, as it was sealed with baptism in his name and through a ceremonial meal in his memory. That was how the church initially took shape.

The meaning of 'church'

From earliest times until the present the church has been, as it still is, the fellowship of those who believe in Christ, the fellowship of those who have committed themselves to the person and cause of Christ and attest it as hope for all men and women. Its very name shows the degree to which the church is obligated to its Lord's cause. In the Germanic languages ('church', 'Kirche') the name is derived from the Greek kyriake = belonging to the Kyrios, Lord, and means the house or the community of the Lord. In the Romance languages (ecclesia, iglesia, chiesa, église) it derives from the Greek word ekklesia, which is also used in the New Testament, or the Hebrew word *qahal*, and means 'assembly' (of God). Here the reference is to both the process of assembling and the assembled community.

This establishes the norm once and for all: the original meaning of *ekklesia*, 'church', was not a hyper-organization of spiritual functionaries, detached from the concrete assembly. It denoted a community gathering at a particular place at a particular time for a particular action, a local church, though with the other local churches it formed a comprehensive community, the whole church. According to the New Testament, every individual local community is given what it needs for human salvation: the gospel to proclaim, baptism as a rite of initiation, the celebration of a meal in grateful remembrance, the various charisms and ministries. Thus every local church makes the whole church fully present; indeed it may understand itself – in the language of the New Testament – as people of God, body of Christ, and building of the Spirit.

Assembly, house, community, church of Jesus Christ. That means that the origin and the name carry with them an obligation: the church has to serve the cause of Jesus Christ. Where the church does not realize the cause of Jesus Christ, or distorts it, it sins against its being and loses that being. We have already recognized to some degree what Jesus intended with his proclamation of the kingdom and will of God and the salvation of men and women. But in view of the history of the Catholic Church, our perspective should be focused more sharply by a question which is hardly ever asked: Was this Jesus, to whom the Catholic Church constantly appeals, really catholic?

Was Jesus catholic?

Catholics who think along traditional lines usually tacitly presuppose that he was. The Catholic Church has always been fundamentally what it is today, the thinking goes, and what the Catholic Church has always said and intended is what originally Jesus Christ himself said and intended. So, in principle, Jesus himself would already have been a Catholic...

But is this Christian church which is so successful, this greatest and most powerful of Christian churches, right in appealing to Jesus? Or is this hierarchical church proudly appealing to someone who would possibly have turned against it? By way of experiment, is it possible to imagine Jesus of Nazareth at a papal mass in St Peter's, Rome? Or would people there perhaps use the same words as Dostoevsky's Grand Inquisitor: 'Why do you come to disturb us?'

At any rate, we must never forget what the sources are unanimous in reporting. Through his words and actions, this man from Nazareth became involved in a dangerous conflict with the ruling forces of his time. Not with the people, but with the official religious authorities, with the hierarchy, which (in a legal process which is no longer clear to us today) handed him over to the Roman governor and thus to his death. Such a thing is of course no longer conceivable. Or is it? Even in today's Catholic Church, might Jesus have become involved in dangerous conflicts if he so radically put in question the dominant religious circles and cliques and the traditional religious practices of so many pious and fundamentalist Catholics? What if he even initiated a public protest action against the way in which piety was practised in the sanctuary of the priests and the high priest and identified himself with the concerns of a 'popular church movement from below'?

Or is all that a grotesque idea? A pure anachronism? Be this as it may, it is no anachronism to claim that Jesus was anything but the representative of a patriarchal hierarchy.

One who relativized the 'fathers' and their traditions and even called women to his circle of disciples cannot be claimed in support of a patriarchalism which is hostile to women.

One who praised marriage and nowhere made celibacy a condition of discipleship, a man whose first disciples were all married and remained so (Paul claims that he is an exception), cannot serve as the authority for a rule that clergy shall be celibate.

One who served his disciples at table and required that 'the highest shall be the servant (at table) of all' can hardly have desired aristocratic or even monarchical structures for his community of disciples.

Rather, Jesus radiated a 'democratic' spirit in the best sense of the word. This was matched by a 'people' (Greek *demos*) of those who are free (no dominating institution, even a Grand Inquisition) and in principle equal (not a church characterized by class, caste, race or office), of brothers and sisters (not a regiment of men and a cult of persons). This was the original Christian 'liberty, equality and fraternity'. But did not the original community already clearly have a hierarchical structure with apostles as pillars and Peter as a rock?

The earliest church

Beyond doubt there were apostles in the earliest community. But over and above the Twelve, which Jesus himself chose as a symbol, all those who preached the message of Christ and founded communities as primal witnesses and primal messengers were apostles. Alongside them, however, other figures are also mentioned as early as the letters of Paul: prophets and prophetesses, who delivered inspired messages, and teachers, evangelists and helpers of very different kinds, men and women.

May we not speak of 'offices' in the original church? No, because the secular term office (*arche* and similar Greek words) is nowhere used for these different church ministries and callings. One realizes why. 'Office' indicates a relationship of domination. Instead, in earliest Christianity a term was used for which Jesus himself set the standard when he said: 'let the leader become as one who serves' (Luke 22.26; this saying has been handed down in six variants). Rather than talking about office, people spoke of *diakonia*, service, originally as in serving at table. So this was a word with connotations of inferiority, which could not evoke any kind of associations with any form of authority, rule, dignity or position of power. Certainly there was also authority and power in the primitive church, but in the spirit of that saying of Jesus it was not to be set up for the purposes of rule (and for acquiring and preserving privileges), but only for service and the well-being of all.

Thus what we have is 'service of the church' and not 'hierarchy'. Slowly the word has got around in the Catholic Church of our day that this term means 'holy rule'. And of course it would have been the last term people would have used to denote service in the church. For what was more to be avoided, following the example of Jesus, than any style of rule and any allure of rule, however much it was dressed up as 'holy' in a sacral way? The unfortunate term 'hierarchy' was introduced only five hundred years after Christ, by an unknown theologian who hid behind the mask of Paul's disciple Dionysius.

The present-day word 'priest' (*Priester, prêtre, prete, presbitero*) is ambiguous. In the New Testament it is certainly used for dignitaries of the other religions in the religious and cultic sense of the priest who offers sacrifices (*hiereus*, *sacerdos*), but never for those who serve in the Christian communities. Here, rather, the word 'presbyter', 'elder', is used; only in the new languages is that similarly rendered 'priest'. Later we find the *'presbyter parochianus'*, from which the Italian word *parocco* and the German word *Pfarrer* come. There were elders at the head of every Jewish community, from time immemorial. Thus it is probable that from as early as the 40s, the Christian community in Jerusalem had its own elders; at the same time it possibly also adopted the laying on of hands which came from the Jewish tradition: ordination for the authoritative sending of a specific member of the community for a specific ministry.

However, we cannot establish historically whether there was a distinctive constitution of elders in Jerusalem which claimed to have jurisdiction over the local church and then the church as a whole. At any rate, we cannot discover whether this was the case before the departure of Peter, and the time when James took over the leadership of the earliest Jerusalem community. But what about this Peter, who very soon takes on a towering significance for the Catholic Church?

Peter

The question here is not what became of Peter (we shall be concerned with that later) but what Peter originally was: the role of Peter in the earliest community. According to the New Testament sources, three things are indisputably certain.
1. Already during Jesus's public activity, the fisherman Simon, to whom Jesus perhaps gave the nickname 'the rock' (Aramaic 'Cepha', Greek 'Peter'), was the spokesman of the

disciples. However, he was the first among equals, and his failure to understand, his faint-heartedness, and finally his flight are reported unsparingly in the Gospels. Only Luke's Gospel and Acts of the Apostles idealize him and keep quiet about Jesus's saying to Peter when Peter wants to deter him from his mission: 'Get away from me, Satan' (Mark 8.33; Matthew 16.23).

2. After Mary Magdalene and the women, Peter was one of the first witnesses of the resurrection of Jesus. In the light of his Easter witness he could be regarded as the 'rock' of the church. But today even Catholic New Testament scholars accept that the famous saying about Peter as the rock on which Jesus will build his church (Matthew 16.18f.: the statement is in the future tense), and of which the other Gospels know nothing, is not a saying of the earthly Jesus but was composed after Easter by the Palestinian community, or later by Matthew's community.

3. Peter was undoubtedly the leader of the earliest Jerusalem community: not, however – and this is decisive – alone, but together with the group of Twelve and later in the group of the three 'pillars' (Galatians 2.9): James (whom Paul in his letters puts in first place), Peter and John. Later Peter is responsible for the proclamation of Christ among his fellow Jews bound to the sacred law of Moses.

In the earliest church Peter doubtless had a special authority; however, he did not possess it alone, but always collegially with others. He was far removed from being a spiritual monarch, even a sole ruler. There is no trace of any exclusive, quasi-monarchical authority as leader. But, at the end of his life, was not Peter in Rome – indeed, was he not Bishop of Rome?

Was Peter in the then-capital of the world, whose church and bishop were later to claim legal primacy throughout the church by appealing to the fisherman from Galilee? This is not an unimportant question in view of the later development of the Catholic Church. Given the existing sources, there is broad agreement among professional scholars on the following three points:

1. Peter was certainly in Antioch, where there was a dispute with Paul over the application of the Jewish law. Possibly he was also in Corinth, where there was evidently a party which claimed allegiance to Cephas, i.e., Peter. But we do not read anywhere in the New Testament that Peter was in Rome.

2. Far less is there any evidence of a successor to Peter (also in Rome) in the New Testament. In any case, the logic of the saying about the rock tends to tell against it: Peter's faith in Christ (and not the faith of any successor) was to be, and remain, the constant foundation of the church.

3. Still, the 'Letter of Clement', around AD 90, and Bishop Ignatius of Antioch, around 110, already attest a stay of Peter in Rome and his martyrdom there. This tradition is therefore old, and above all it is unanimous and unrivalled: at the end of his life, Peter was in Rome and probably suffered a martyr's death in the course of the Neronian persecution. However, archaeology has not been able to identify his tomb under the present Vatican basilica.

For a long time there has been a consensus among scholars: even Protestant theologians now affirm that Peter suffered a martyr's death in Rome. Conversely, however, Catholic theologians concede that there is no reliable evidence that Peter was ever in charge of the church of Rome as supreme head or bishop. In any case the monarchical episcopate was introduced to Rome relatively late. And here we should not forget the matter of qualifications: unlike Paul, who presumably suffered martyrdom in Rome at the same time, Peter was not an educated Roman citizen (*civis Romanus*, with a perfect command of the Greek language and Greek conceptuality), but an uneducated Galilean Jew.

A fellowship made up of Jews

Rome is the city which contains the tombs of the two chief apostles. But does that make it the mother of all churches? To the present day the gigantic inscription on the Lateran basilica, the original church of the Bishop of Rome, runs: *Omnium urbis et orbis ecclesiarum mater et caput* – 'Head and Mother of All Churches of the City and the Earth'. However, indisputably, it was not Rome but Jerusalem that was the head and mother community of the first Christianity. And the history of the earliest community was not a history of Romans and Greeks but a history of born Jews, whether they spoke Aramaic or, as was often the case in the Hellenistic culture of Palestine, Greek. These Jews who followed Jesus handed on to the church that was coming into being Jewish language, ideas and theology, and thus left an indelible stamp on the whole of Christianity.

Theirs is the history of lower classes without the slightest political or economic power, including a great many women. Following the example of Jesus, there was particular openness to the poor, the oppressed, the wretched, the desperate, those who were discriminated against and outcast. Not all were poor in the financial sense; there were those (like Peter himself) who had houses; some later made them available for assemblies. In accordance with Jesus's message there was a call for inner freedom from possessions, and generosity; certainly there were cases where possessions were voluntarily renounced. However the ideal picture painted by the evangelist Luke two decades later was not backed up by other witnesses: there was no general renunciation of property in the earliest community. In expectation of the coming kingdom of God – which had already dawned in the raising of Jesus to life and in the experience of the Spirit of God – there was no requirement to dispose of property, but there was a call to help the needy and to share possessions. So this was no sharing of goods in a communistic way, but more a community which was showing social solidarity.

The earliest Christian community did not want in any way to part company with the Jewish community or nation, but to remain integrated into Judaism. After all, it shared with all Jews belief in the one God ('Shema Israel') and held firm to the Holy Scriptures (Tenach). People also visited the temple, prayed the psalms and continued to observe the Mosaic ritual law (*halakhah*): above all circumcision, the sabbath and festivals, and the regulations relating to cleanliness and food. The one thing that they would not allow to be taken from them in any way was belief in Jesus, the 'Messiah', Greek *Christos*. The whole life of these 'Jew Christians', their thought and practice, centred on him, the one who was crucified and yet was alive. For them, Jesus's proclamation of the kingdom became a proclamation of Jesus as the Messiah, and the gospel preached by Jesus became the gospel about Jesus Christ. One visibly belonged to the faith community of those who believed in Christ if one was baptized in the name of Jesus and took part in the thanksgiving meal in memory of him. But how did the break between Jews and Christians come about?

The break between Jews and Christians

Persecutions and executions made a decisive contribution to the alienation: at a very early stage the executions first of the Hellenistic Jewish-Christian Stephen; then of James the son of Zebedee, one of the Twelve (in AD 43); and above all that of James 'the brother of the Lord', one of Jesus's four brothers and head of the Jerusalem community after the departure of Peter (AD 62). Finally Paul, the apostle to the Gentiles, was arrested in Jerusalem and executed in Rome after a trial lasting two years (AD 64).

However, the definitive break was brought about after the destruction of the second temple by the Romans in AD 70 by a Jewish 'council' in Jamnia (near Jaffa) which was composed of Pharisees: this was the formal excommunication of the Christians, a 'curse on heretics', which was to be repeated at the beginning of every synagogue service. It had serious social consequences. If, like me, one does not spare the Catholic Church criticism, it must also be said quite unmistakably that the anti-Judaism which can already be found among the Jewish Christians, and which in a lamentable way is already recorded in the Gospels of Matthew and John, had its decisive roots in the persecution of Christians and their exclusion from the synagogue. The excommunication of the Christians by the Pharisaic establishment preceded all persecutions of Jews by Christians.

However, the great question now is: How did the small Jewish-Christian church which began in Palestine become the great church of the whole 'ecumene', the whole of the then 'inhabited earth', the *ecclesia catholica*? Beyond doubt the apostle Paul was a key figure for the paradigm change from Jewish Christianity (partly Aramaic-speaking, partly Greek-speaking) to Gentile Christianity (initially Greek-speaking, then Latin-speaking).

II   *The Early Catholic Church*

The word 'Christian' was first used in Antioch in Syria (present-day Antakya). Antioch was the third most important city in the Roman empire after Rome and Alexandria, at the junction of the land routes between Asia Minor, Mesopotamia and Egypt. Even before Paul, the Hellenistic Jewish Christians who fled from Jerusalem after the martyrdom of Stephen addressed their preaching directly to the Gentiles in Antioch. And so there the 'Christians' (Greek *Christianoi* = 'Christ people') founded the first mixed community made up both of born Jews and born Gentiles.

Whereas the Jesus movement had been at home in a rural setting, Christianity now became an urban phenomenon: people no longer spoke Aramaic/Hebrew, but common Greek (*koine* Greek), the vernacular in the Roman empire. Thus Antioch became the centre of the mission to the Gentiles. From here, too, the apostle Paul undertook his bold and hazardous missionary journeys around the Eastern Mediterranean.

The word 'catholic' (Greek *katholikos* = 'related to the whole', 'general') is not used anywhere in the New Testament. Nowhere is the 'church' called 'catholic'. The expression 'catholic church' was used for the first time by Ignatius, the Bishop of Antioch, in his letter to the community in Smyrna (8.2). Here 'catholic church' simply means the 'whole' church – as distinct from the individual local churches. This word denotes a comprehensive universal church, the reality of which was now being experi-

25

enced increasingly clearly; later it would be called in Latin the *ecclesia catholica* or *universalis*.

Paul

The history of early Christianity would doubtless have taken another course without the conversion of the Pharisee Saul from Tarsus, a man loyal to the Jewish law, to faith in Jesus Christ. The persecutor of the young Christian community saw Jesus alive in a vision and he felt called by him as an 'apostle', as an 'authorized envoy', to proclaim him, the Messiah of Israel, as Messiah/Christ to the whole world, made up of Jews and Gentiles. Paul was not the real founder of Christianity – though this is constantly asserted by those who will not be taught. In many respects Paul stood in continuity with the preaching of Jesus, but in the light of Jesus's death and new life he transformed it in a brilliant way with the help of both Jewish and Hellenistic concepts and ideas.

Paul not only shared faith in Jesus as the Messiah, the Christ of God, with the Jewish Christians, who wanted to retain the Mosaic ritual law, but also engaged in practical discipleship: he administered baptism in the name of Jesus and celebrated the ceremonial meal in his memory. In other words, Paul took over the original Christian 'substance of faith' and also aspired to transmit it to the Gentile Christians.

Like his 'Lord Jesus' Paul was firmly convinced that the sinful person (like the tax collector in the temple) was justified by God on the basis of an unconditional trust, without having earned such grace by his own achievements or being able to earn it by pious works of the law. Certainly the apostle to the Gentiles in no way wanted to abolish the Jewish ritual law, the *halakhah*;

among Jews he observed the law. But Paul would neither pre-
scribe it nor demonstrate it to the Gentiles: to the Jews he
wanted to be a Jew, but to those 'outside the law' he wanted to
be one 'outside the law'. Indeed, access to faith in the universal
God of Israel was to be made possible for the Gentiles without
their previously submitting to circumcision, and without their
having to observe all the Jewish commandments relating to
cleanness, the prescriptions of the *halakhah* relating to food
and to the sabbath, which alienated them. Paul established that
a Gentile could become a Christian without previously going
over to Judaism, without having to fulfil the 'works of the law'.

With his programme and his restless activity, in intellectual
matters and theology as well as in missionary work and church
politics, the apostle had a resounding success with his mission
to the Gentiles. Only in this way could a real inculturation of
the Christian message come about in the world of Hellenistic
culture; only in this way could the little Jewish 'sect' become a
world religion which brought together East and West. Despite
its universal monotheism, Judaism, which also engaged in an
intensive mission to the Gentiles, in Antioch in particular,
did not become the universal religion of humankind; it was
Christianity which most approached that status, and the little
church of its beginnings became the *ecclesia catholica*. To this
extent it is no exaggeration to say that there would have been
no Catholic Church without Paul.

The Pauline churches

Bishops of the Catholic Church (like those of the Anglican and
Orthodox Churches) are fond of calling themselves 'successors
of the apostles'. The presbyteral-episcopal constitution of the

church is said to have been 'instituted by Jesus Christ', even to be a 'divine institution' and therefore unchangeable 'divine law' (*iuris divini*). However, it is not as simple as that. A careful investigation of the New Testament sources in the last hundred years has shown that this church constitution, centred on the bishop, is by no means willed by God or given by Christ, but is the result of a long and problematical historical development. It is human work and therefore, in principle, can be changed.

Any reader of the Bible can see from the earliest documents of the New Testament, those letters of the apostle Paul of which the authenticity is undisputed, that there is not a word in them about a legal institution of the church (even on the basis of Paul's 'apostolic authority'). In contrast to the account in Luke's later Acts of the Apostles and the even later 'early catholic' Pastoral Epistles (addressed to Timothy and Titus), in the Pauline communities there was neither a monarchical episcopate nor a presbyterate nor an ordination by the laying on of hands.

And yet Paul was convinced that his Gentile Christian churches were in their way complete and well-equipped churches, which did not lack anything essential; the non-episcopal, 'congregationalist' churches of a later period would appeal to this. The Pauline churches were in fact largely communities with free charismatic ministries. According to Paul, all Christians have their quite personal calling, their own gift of the Spirit, their special 'charism' for service to the community. Thus, in his churches, there was a whole series of different and also quite everyday ministries and functions: for preaching, giving help and leading the community.

When Paul lists those involved in functions and ministries in the church, of course the apostles are fundamental; as the first witnesses and messengers, they proclaimed the message of

Christ and founded churches. Second come the prophets and thirdly the teachers. Well down in his list follows the 'provision of help' and only in penultimate place the 'gifts of leadership', which can be organized in very different ways in different communities: evidently these functions of the communities are instituted in an autonomous way, depending on the situation. Women, especially well-to-do women, who made their houses available for meetings and worship, often played the leading role here. The Acts of the Apostles makes mention of prophetesses, and Paul even of women apostles: 'Junia, prominent among the apostles' (Romans 16.7). In later editions of the text Junia was turned into 'Junias', a man!

In his first letter to the community of Corinth, Paul thinks it quite normal that the eucharist is celebrated there without him and without anyone who has been appointed to an office, though at the same time it is taken for granted that a certain order should be observed. According to the earliest community order, the Didache ('Teaching' of the apostles, around AD 100), above all prophets and teachers celebrate the eucharist and only after them elected bishops and deacons. The community of Antioch was clearly led not by *episkopoi* (bishops) and presbyters, but by prophets and teachers. In Rome, too, at the time when Paul wrote his letter to the Romans, there was evidently as yet no community order with *episkopoi*. That makes the question of how a hierarchy came into being all the more interesting.

The birth of the Catholic hierarchy

After the death of the apostle Paul a degree of institutionalization was unavoidable, even in his communities. In the Palestinian tradition it began at an early stage with the adoption of the college of elders and the rite of laying on of hands. But at the end of the New Testament period there was still a great diversity of community constitutions and forms of serving ministries. And every community, indeed every member of a community, had to stand in the 'apostolic succession' – in accordance with the message and action of the apostles. Not only just a few people, but the whole church was an 'apostolic church', as it would be called in the creed.

It cannot be verified that the bishops are 'successors of the apostles' in the direct and exclusive sense. It is historically impossible to find in the initial phase of Christianity an unbroken chain of 'laying on of hands' from the apostles to the present-day bishops. Historically, rather, it can be demonstrated that in a first post-apostolic phase local presbyter-bishops became established alongside prophets, teachers and other ministries as the sole leaders of the Christian communities (and also at the celebration of the eucharist); thus a division between 'clergy' and 'laity' took place at an early stage. In a further phase the monarchical episcopate of an individual bishop increasingly displaced a plurality of presbyter bishops in a city and later throughout the region of a church. In Antioch, around 110, with Bishop Ignatius there came into being the order of three offices which became customary all over the empire: bishop, presbyter and deacon. The eucharist could no longer be celebrated without a bishop. The division between 'clergy' and 'people' was now a fact.

But it is striking that even Ignatius, this defender and ideologue of the monarchical episcopate, did not address a bishop in his letter to the Roman community, any more than Paul did. And there was no mention of a bishop in Rome in any other of the earliest sources like the 'Letter of Clement' (around 90). However, from the beginning the Roman community showed that it had a high sense of itself and enjoyed general respect: not only because it was the community of the imperial capital, large, prosperous and famed for its charitable activity (Ignatius remarked that it had the 'primacy of love'), but also because it was the undisputed location of the tombs of the two main apostles Peter and Paul. However, the earliest list of bishops in the second-century church father Irenaeus of Lyons, according to which Peter and Paul transferred the ministry of *episkopos* to a certain Linus, is a second-century forgery. A monarchical episcopate can be demonstrated for Rome only from around the middle of the second century (Bishop Anicetus).

Thus the presbyteral-episcopal church constitution is not based on any institution by Jesus Christ and can in no way be seen as absolutely intrinsic to Christianity, using as a measure the words of Jesus himself, the earliest community and the charismatic constitution of the Pauline churches. But it was not apostasy either, and beyond dispute it was of great pastoral use. With good reason it became the norm in the early *ecclesia catholica*. All in all it was a meaningful historical development which gave the Christian communities both continuity in time and coherence in space, or, as one could also put it, catholicity in time and space. So it is not to be criticized as long as it is used in the spirit of the gospel, for the benefit of men and women and not to preserve and idolize the power of the 'hierarchs'. In a word, the succession of bishops is functional rather than historical; the activity of bishops is rooted in the preaching of the gospel and they should support the other charisms rather than 'quench' them. In particular, prophets and teachers had their own authority.

A persecuted minority endures

At the beginning of the second century after the birth of Christ hardly anyone in the Roman empire was likely to have given the Catholic Church then coming into being a chance of establishing itself in the Graeco-Roman world, with its numerous religions and philosophies, and its thousands upon thousands of temples and theatres, its arenas and gymnasia. However, the church community made up of Jews was now one of Jews and Gentiles, and it was well on the way to becoming a community of Gentiles alone.

What happened to the Jewish Christians? Important parts of the earliest community emigrated from Jerusalem to Trans-jordan (Pella) as early as AD 66, after the execution of James, the leader of their community – in other words, before the outbreak of the war between the Jews and Rome. After a further Jewish rebellion, with the complete destruction of Jerusalem and the expulsion of all the Jews, the fateful year 135 also brought about the end of the Jewish-Christian community of Jerusalem and its dominant position in the early church. Soon Jewish Christianity and its christology with a Jewish stamp, along with its observance of the law, was perceived by the Gentile Christian church as merely a sect surviving from an earlier stage. Very soon it was felt to be heretical. However, where these Jewish Christians preserved the oldest beliefs and patterns of life, they represented the legitimate heirs of early Christianity. Sadly, though, this tradition was later to get distorted and lost, in Manichaeism and probably also in Islam.

Instead of Jerusalem, Rome was now the centre and leading church of Christianity. Initially Greek was dominant even in the liturgy, and Latin became definitive only from the middle of the fourth century on. Initially the young church was under an unfavourable star and Christians were persecuted. In AD 64 the Emperor Nero had numerous Christians executed in a cruel way as scapegoats for a great fire in Rome which he himself had staged. This was a fatal precedent: from then on, one could be condemned simply for being a Christian. There was a second persecution under the Emperor Domitian (81–96); the 'oath' by the emperor was declared compulsory. However, the Christians refused to offer worship to the emperor and the state gods because of their belief in the one God. But refusal to participate in the state cult and to think as the state did was a crime against the state (crimen laesae Romanae religionis).

Still, before AD 250 the persecutions were not systematic and uninterrupted, but limited, local, erratic, sporadic. Christians continued to celebrate their eucharist as before in their private houses, and not, as would later be suggested, in the catacombs. But being a Christian meant in principle being ready to 'martyrein', to 'bear witness' to Christian belief: through being discriminated against, through suffering, torture, indeed death. This was what, among many others, bishops Ignatius of Antioch and Polycarp of Smyrna did, and also women like Blandina, Perpetua and Felicitas: in the process, as was usual, the women were made available for prostitution. Thus 'martyr' was used as a name for 'bearing witness with one's blood'; 'confessor' was the name given to those who bravely survived the persecution. The Christian was to endure the ultimate fate of martyrdom, but not to seek it.

But despite all the persecutions, the number of Christians inexorably grew. And it was the persecutions which – leaving aside the letters of Paul – provoked early Christian theology. Ignatius, Polycarp and other 'apostolic fathers' composed writings merely

for use within the church (usually 'letters'). However, in the face
of all the pagan misunderstandings, attacks and calumniations,
now public 'apologias' became necessary, defensive writings
sometimes addressed to the emperor. They had little impact in
the wider world of politics, but their influence within the church
was immense. These 'apologists', who all wrote in Greek, were
the first Christian literary figures to present Christianity as
credible to all interested parties in Hellenistic terms, views and
methods which could generally be understood. In so doing they
showed themselves to be the first Christian theologians, who
sparked off in the catholic church an impetus towards Hellenization which is still tangible in the formulations of faith.

We may recall only the most educated of the apologists, Justin,
who was born in Palestine and then worked publicly in Rome
(he was executed in 165). He knew how to make intelligent use
in his arguments of Platonic metaphysics, Stoic ethics and the
Hellenistic criticism of myths in order to show up pagan polytheism and myth (immoral stories about the gods) and worship
(bloody sacrifices, the veneration of animals) as superstition,
indeed the work of demons, and to claim philosophers like
Heraclitus and Socrates as 'Christians before Christ'. Christianity was presented as the true philosophy. This represented
a first philosophical and theological synthesis of a universal,
catholic character. At its centre was the divine 'Logos', that
eternal 'word' implanted in every human being as the 'seed of
truth', which illuminated the prophets of Israel and also the wise
men of Greece, and finally took human form in Jesus Christ.

This was a great conception with a future, and in the first half
of the third century it was adopted above all by the Alexandrian
Origen, the only real genius among the Greek church fathers.
This Greek, with a comprehensive education and tremendous
creativity, became the inventor of theology as a science; he was

driven by passion to achieve a definitive reconciliation between Christianity and the Greek world, the transcendence and abolition of Greek culture in Christianity.

Origen understood the whole of human history as a grandiose educational process leading continuously upwards, as God's own 'pedagogy' with the human race. The image of God which in human beings was obscured by guilt and sin was restored by the divine art of education in Christ. In this way Christianity was presented as the most perfect of all religions: the incarnation of God ultimately led on to the divinization of human beings. This way of thinking was utterly Hellenistic, and also brought about a shift in emphasis of which Christians at the time were barely aware: from the cross and the resurrection of Jesus to the incarnation and pre-existence of the Logos and Son of God.

The negative effects of this Hellenization of Christian preaching were unmistakable. In accordance with its Hebraic origins, the 'truth' of Christianity was not to be 'seen', or 'theorized on'; rather, it was to be 'done', 'practised'. Thus, in the Gospel of John, Jesus Christ is called 'the way, the truth and the life' (14.6). The Christian concept of truth was originally not contemplative and theoretical, like the Greek concept, but operative and practical.

But in Hellenistic Christianity the arguments turned less and less on the practical discipleship of Christ and more on the acceptance of a revealed teaching – about God and Jesus Christ, God and the world. And the new Logos christology increasingly forced the Jesus of history into the background in favour of a doctrine and finally a church dogma of the 'incarnate God'. Whereas in Judaism, from Jesus's time to the present day, there have been arguments about the correct practice of the law, in

Hellenized Christianity the arguments have been increasingly about the 'right', the 'orthodox' truth of faith.

No wonder that now the christological heresies became increasingly numerous and that more and more often it was thought necessary to note deviations from the truth of the universal, catholic church – now also explicitly called the 'great church'. The term 'catholic' (= whole, universal, all-embracing), which originally was not polemical in any way, was now increasingly focused polemically on having a 'true belief', on being 'orthodox'.

In the second century, the spiritual argument was concentrated on that great religious movement of late antiquity which promised a spiritual elite 'gnosis', i.e., knowledge, a redemptive 'knowledge' of the origin of evil in the world and of the divine spark of life which has descended into the human body and needs to be freed so that it can rise again from the evil world of matter into the divine world of light. It was a form of thought and an attitude which many people found fascinating.

But bishops, theologians and theologian bishops like Irenaeus of Lyons defended the simple 'faith' (Greek *pistis*) of the Christian community. They defended the simple Gospels, commandments and rites in the face of the allegedly higher, purely spiritual 'knowledge' which rested on particular 'revelations', myths, secret traditions and world-systems, combined itself with mysterious rituals and magical procedures, and was marked by a syncretistic mythologization and hostility to the world, matter and the body.

The 'catholic' or mainstream church refused to accept that Gnostic speculations and practices might make it possible for Christianity to adopt the existing syncretistic religious system of the state, in which all and everything had a place. On the contrary, it defended its belief by laying down clear standards (Greek *kanon*) of what was Christian. There were above all three regulative norms which, to the present day, are meant to mark out the 'catholic' church as opposed to 'heretical' or schismatic movements.

The first standard was the summary creed which was customary at baptism. This now became the normative rule of faith or truth, which could be supplemented with definitions or dogmas that marked out limits of right, 'orthodox', belief.

The second standard was the eventual establishment of a New Testament canon of scripture, based on the Hebrew Bible, for the writings which were recognized by the church and allowed in the liturgy.

The third standard was the office of *episkopos* or bishop. This was originally concerned more with organization (the 'economy' of the church), but now became the episcopal teaching office: a decision on the correct 'apostolic' teaching was entrusted to bishops on the basis of the 'apostolic succession'. Lists of bishops and synods of bishops, indeed 'the tradition', generally became increasingly important, and the power of the bishops grew ever greater. The bishops displaced the charismatic teachers, and also the prophets – and the prophetesses.

Unfortunately the establishment of hierarchical structures, in particular, prevented the true emancipation of women and still does. Certainly the Greek church fathers kept emphasizing that men and women had equal status, both being created in the image of God. But at the same time hostility to sexuality – a general phenomenon in late antiquity – took on a particular stamp in Christianity. The earliest Christian ethos of 'equality' asserted itself predominantly in the private sphere, but education, a lofty Hellenistic ideal, was usually withheld from women.

Male domination established itself completely, especially in the sphere of the sacral. Countless theologians and bishops advocated the inferiority of the feminine and – contrary to all that was allowed and desired in the earliest church – called for the exclusion of women from holding office in the church. There is no question that women were more intensively involved in the early dissemination of Christianity than the sources, with their male-centred colouring, at first suggest. Consequently present-day women's studies are making great efforts to rediscover the early Christian women who were martyrs, prophetesses and teachers and also to see a contribution to the history of the emancipation of women in what were then by no means regressive forms of life, but alternatives to marriage (virginity, widowhood).

However, despite all the criticism, the fact cannot be overlooked that with the three standards mentioned above the Catholic Church created a structure for theology and organization and with it a very resistant inner order – but at the expense of the original freedom and multiplicity. Centuries later the Reformation was to put in question the third standard (the office of bishop); the Enlightenment was to put in question the second standard (the canon of scripture) and ultimately also the first (the rule of faith). However, to the present day, all three standards have continued to be important for all churches which lay claim to some form of catholicity, though their meanings have been revised. But what must be more important for a religious movement than any institutions and constitutions is its spiritual and moral power, and in the early centuries the church was by no means lacking in this.

It is true that in the first centuries Christians did not question such deeply rooted institutions as slavery, and 'only' called for a brotherly treatment of slaves, who now could also become priests, deacons, and indeed in the case of the freeman Callistus, even Bishop of Rome. At first the church also had reservations about military service: converts did not need to leave the army, but clergy above all were to abstain from military service, as from other occupations which caused offence (gladiator, actor).

But only the ignorant or the malicious could claim that Christianity had not changed the world for the better. First of all the resolute assertion by Christians of belief in the one God, while showing complete loyalty to the state, finally overcame the absolutizing of political power and the divinization of the ruler. In the face of the collapse of morals in the great cities of the later period of the empire, the church indefatigably inculcated the elementary commandments of the God of Israel. Thus Christianity proved to be a moral power which deeply shaped society in a long process of transformation.

More recent studies (see the works of Peter Brown) have shown how, above all, a new ethical ideal was worked out in the early church: action not simply in accordance with law, custom and class morality, but arising out of a pure, undivided, simple heart – looking towards Christ and fellow men and women. In paganism it was part of the morality of the upper classes to lavish large sums of money on festivals for 'their' city, for its glory and their own, for 'bread and circuses' (*panem et circenses*). But now, in Christianity, it was to be the everyday morality of those who were better off than others to support the poor and suffering in continuous regular solidarity. And there was no lack of such people in late antiquity.

What was amazing and attractive to many outsiders was the social cohesion of Christians as expressed, above all, in worship: 'brothers' and 'sisters', with no distinctions of class, race and education, could take part in the eucharist. Extraordinarily generous voluntary gifts were brought, usually during worship. Administered and distributed by the bishop, they made it possible to provide welfare for the poor, the sick, orphans and widows, travellers, those in prison, the needy and the aged. To this degree right living (ortho-praxy) was more important in the concrete everyday life of the communities than right teaching (ortho-doxy). At any rate, this was a main reason for the unexpected success of Christianity.

What Henry Chadwick has called the 'paradox of Christianity' shows itself in this gentle revolution which won through in the Roman empire. A revolutionary religious movement 'from below', with no conscious political ideology, eventually conquered society at every level and continued to show itself indifferent to the balance of power in this world.

However, the world was to change – though only after what were now persecutions throughout the empire, which in the second half of the third century under the emperors Decius and Valerian were no longer sporadic and regional, but universal. The death penalty was imposed on bishops, presbyters and deacons, and also on Christian senators and knights; all church buildings and burial places were confiscated. Yet all the persecutions – including the last under Diocletian at the beginning of the fourth century – proved to be a fiasco.

The more spiritual and philosophical form of worship of God, without bloody sacrifices, without statues of gods, incense and temple, increasingly also found approval among educated and well-to-do people, even at the imperial court and in the army. It was above all the theologian Origen from whom so many people learned. With his combination of faith and knowledge, theology and philosophy, he worked out that theological change which made possible the cultural change – the combination of Christianity and Greek culture. And this cultural change in turn furthered the political change: the alliance of church and state. No one could have any inkling that only fifty years after Origen's arrest and torture (in the end the famous man was not burned at the stake, the punishment with which he had been threatened), there would be a revolution in world history.

III   *The Imperial Catholic Church*

A universal religion for the universal empire

The fourth century saw one of the great revolutions in world events: the recognition of Christianity by the Roman empire. Though not himself a Christian, Constantine attributed to the God of the Christians and the sign of the cross, which he had seen in a dream the night before, the victory in the decisive battle which was to bring him to the imperial throne. To the great delight of Christians, in AD 313 this cool master of *realpolitik*, with his co-regent Licinius, granted unlimited freedom of religion to the whole empire. In 315 the punishment of crucifixion was abolished, and in 321 Sunday was introduced as a legal festival and the church was allowed to accept legacies. In 325 Constantine became sole ruler of the Roman empire and convened the first ecumenical council. It was held in his residence at Nicaea, east of Byzantium.

Why did the Christian church assert itself, contrary to all expectations, in the world of late antiquity, and finally become established? There is no single explanation. Many factors have emerged:

– The comprehensive organization of the church, with its solid roots, and the manifold forms of charitable help to the many who were poor and in distress;

– Christian monotheism which commended itself as the progressive and enlightened position in the face of polytheism, with its wealth of myths;

– The lofty ethic which, tested by ascetics and martyrs to the point of death, shows itself to be superior to pagan morality;

– Clear answers to problems like guilt and atonement, dying and immortality;

– And, with all this, a wide-ranging assimilation to Hellenistic-Roman society.

Once the freedom of religion which had been so long desired was granted, the religious tensions within Christianity which had already been present for so long clearly came to light. They had to do, above all, with a christology interpreted in Hellenistic terms. For the more Jesus as the Son – in contrast to the Jewish-Christian paradigm – was elevated to the same level of being as God the Father, and the relationship between Son and Father came to be described with naturalistic Hellenistic categories and notions, the more difficult it became to reconcile divine Sonship with monotheism. There seemed to be two Gods.

The Alexandrian presbyter Arius now asserted that as Son, Christ was indeed created before all time, but was still a creature. Arius provoked a tremendous controversy which initially shook the Eastern church. When the Emperor Constantine saw a spiritual split threatening the unity of the empire, which had just been united politically under his sole rule, in 325 he convened the council in Nicaea. All the bishops of the empire could, and did, use the imperial postal service to attend.

But it was the emperor who had the say at the council; the Bishop of Rome was not even invited. The emperor convened the imperial synod; he guided it through a bishop whom he appointed and through imperial commissars; he made the resolutions of the council state laws by endorsing them. At the same time he took the opportunity of assimilating the organization of the church to the organization of the state: the church provinces were to correspond with the imperial provinces ('dioceses'), each with a metropolitan and a provincial synod (especially for the election of bishops). Ideologically, the emperor was supported by the 'political theology' of his court bishop, Eusebius of Caesarea.

All of this meant that the empire now had its imperial church. And already, at the first ecumenical council, this imperial church was given its ecumenical creed. This creed became the law of the church and the empire for all churches – everything was now increasingly dominated by the slogan 'One God, one emperor, one empire, one church, one faith'.

According to this faith, Jesus Christ was not created before all time, the view of Arius (who was condemned at the council). Rather, as 'Son' (this more natural term replaced the term 'Logos' which appears in the Gospel of John and features in Greek philosophy) he is 'God of God, light of light, true God of true God, begotten not created, from the substance of the Father'. Constantine himself had the unbiblical word 'of the same substance' (Greek *homo-ousios*, Latin *consubstantialis*) inserted; later it was to cause a great controversy. The subordination of the Son to the one God and Father ('the' God), as was generally taught by Origen and the theologians of the previous period, was now replaced by an essential, substantial equality of the Son with the Father, so that in future it is possible to speak of 'God the Son' and 'God the Father'. The term 'consubstantial', with its background in Greek philosophy, was incomprehensible not only to Jews but also to Jewish Christians.

The state church

Constantine, who was baptized only at the end of his life, pursued a tolerant policy of integration until his death in 337. His sons, who divided the empire, were different, particularly Constantius, the lord of the East. Constantius engaged in a fanatical policy of intolerance against the pagans: the death penalty was threatened for superstition and sacrifice; sacrifices were stopped and the temples were closed. Now Christianity increasingly permeated all political institutions, religious convictions, philosophical thought, art and culture. At the same time, the other religions were often eradicated by force and many works of art were destroyed.

It was the Emperor Theodosius the Great, a strictly orthodox Spaniard, who at the end of the fourth Christian century decreed a general ban on all pagan cults and sacrificial rites and accused those who broke this law of *lèse-majesté* (*laesa majestas*). That made Christianity now formally the state religion, the Catholic Church the state church, and heresy a crime against the state. And even after Arius, there was to be no shortage of new heresies.

What a revolution! In less than a century the persecuted church had become a persecuting church. Its enemies, the 'heretics' (those who 'selected' from the totality of the Catholic faith), were now also the enemies of the empire and were punished accordingly. For the first time Christians killed other Christians because of differences in their views of the faith. This is what happened in Trier in 285: despite many objections, the ascetic and enthusiastic Spanish lay preacher Priscillian was executed for heresy together with six companions. People soon became quite accustomed to this idea.

Above all the Jews came under pressure. The proud Roman Hellenistic state church hardly remembered its own Jewish roots any more. A specifically Christian ecclesiastical anti-Judaism developed out of the pagan state anti-Judaism that already existed. There were many reasons for this: the breaking off of conversations between the church and the synagogue and mutual isolation; the church's exclusive claim to the Hebrew Bible; the crucifixion of Jesus, which was now generally attributed to 'the Jews'; the dispersion of Israel, which was seen as God's just curse on a damned people who were alleged to have broken the covenant with God . . .

Almost exactly a century after Constantine's death, by special state-church laws under Theodosius II, Judaism was removed from the sacral sphere, to which one has access only through the sacraments (i.e., through baptism). The first repressive measures related to mixed marriages, appointment to official posts, the building of synagogues and the recruitment of proselytes. The rabbinic practice of segregation (on religious, 'halakhic' grounds) and the Christian practice of discrimination (on political and theological grounds) influenced each other and in the later Roman empire led to a complete isolation of Judaism.

The Christian state religion was crowned by the dogma of the Trinity. Only now can this term be used, since the second ecumenical council at Constantinople, convened by Theodosius the Great in 381, also defined the identity of substance of the Holy Spirit with the Father and the Son. The creed supplemented by this council, and therefore called the 'Niceno-Constantinopolitan' Creed, is still in use in the Catholic Church today – alongside the brief 'Apostles' Creed'. Centuries later it was to be turned into great music by the greatest composers of Christianity (Bach, Haydn, Mozart, Beethoven in their settings of the mass), so much did it finally come to be taken for granted.

After this council, what the 'three Cappadocians' (from Cappadocia in Asia Minor), Basil the Great, Gregory of Nazianzus and Gregory of Nyssa, had worked out was regarded as the orthodox formula of the Trinity: Trinity = 'a divine being (substance, nature) in three persons' (Father, Son and Spirit). At the fourth ecumenical council at Chalcedon in 451 it was supplemented by the classical christological formula: Jesus Christ = 'one (divine) person in two natures (one divine and one human)'.

But the same council which accepted suggestions for this christological definition from Leo the Great, the Bishop of Rome, again put him in his place. For in a solemn canon the church of Constantinople, which Constantine had founded on the site of Great Byzantium as the new imperial capital in 330, was given the same primacy as ancient Rome. It was known as the 'New Rome'. In neither case was the foundation for this primacy of the council theological; it was political, and associated with the status of the imperial capital. Between 381 and 451 the five classical patriarchates were formed, which still exist today. They had a hierarchy: Rome, the patriarchate of the West; New Rome (Constantinople); Alexandria; Antioch; and – now a good last – Jerusalem.

The Bishop of Rome claims supremacy

After the death of the Emperor Theodosius in 395 the Roman empire was divided into an Eastern empire and a Western empire. For all the historical and symbolic significance of the old imperial capital, Rome, the focal point of the Catholic Church clearly lay in the East, which had a greater population and was stronger economically, culturally and in military terms.

Almost all the 'apostolic' churches, those founded by the apostles, were here. All the ecumenical councils took place here, and the patriarchates, centres of learning and monasteries developed here. Around the middle of the fourth century Latin Christianity still appeared largely to be no more than an appendix to Eastern Roman Byzantine Christianity, which was the spiritual leader. And a good thousand years after the transfer of the imperial capital to the Bosphorus, the empire of the East would continue to hand down the ecumenical paradigm of the early church. After the fall of East Rome (in 1453) it would be passed on to the Slavs: after Constantinople as the 'second Rome', Moscow would finally be the 'third Rome'. To the present day the concrete form of the Russian church – its literature, theology, iconography, piety, constitution – still continues to have a deep Byzantine stamp.

However, for the Christianity of the West, the migration of the Germanic peoples proved to be a decisive revolution. These peoples infiltrated the empire in increasing strength as early as the fourth century, but on 31 December 410 they crossed the frozen Rhine and for the first time captured the unconquered 'eternal Rome'. Now, suddenly, the hour of the Bishop of Rome struck. For at the very moment when ancient culture and civilization was largely sinking in the West along with the Roman state, the bishops of Rome exploited the power vacuum. They did so not so much to fight for their independence from East Rome as to slip away and to build up and exploit their own autocracy. But, it may be asked, was there not a historical, legal, theological, perhaps even biblical basis for the Roman claims to rule?

It could hardly be disputed that the church of the imperial capital – always marked by good organization and charitable activity – also proved to be the stronghold of orthodoxy against Gnosticism and other heresies. It played an important role in the formation of the three standards of what is Catholic that have already been mentioned, both in the formulation of the baptismal creed and the demarcation of the New Testament canon, and in the formation of the apostolic tradition and succession (monuments to Peter and Paul were erected as early as 160). The church of Rome always had a high moral authority.

But there could be no question of a legal primacy – or even of a pre-eminence based on the Bible – of the Roman community or even of the Bishop of Rome in the first centuries. In Rome in particular there was initially no monarchical episcopate, and we know hardly more than the names of the bishops of the first two centuries (the first certain date in papal history is thought to be 222, the beginning of the pontificate of Urban I). The promise to Peter from the Gospel of Matthew (16.18), 'You are Peter, and on this rock I will build my church . . .', which is so central for today's bishops of Rome and which now adorns the interior of St Peter's in huge black letters on a gilt background, is not once quoted in full in any of the Christian literature of the first centuries – apart from a text in the second/third-century African church father Tertullian, and this does not quote the passage in connection with Rome but in connection with Peter.

Only in the middle of the third century did a bishop of Rome by the name of Stephen appeal to the promise to Peter; he did so in a dispute with other churches as to which had the better tradition. However, he was no more successful than was Bishop Victor fifty years previously. Victor attempted to force through in an authoritarian way a uniform, Roman, date for Easter, without respect for the character and independence of the other churches, and was put in his place by the bishops of the East and West, especially by the highly-respected bishop and theologian Irenaeus of Lyons. At that time the rule of one church over the other churches was rejected even in the West.

At the time of the Emperor Constantine it was at any rate clear who had the legal primacy in the church: the emperor. He, the *Pontifex maximus*, the supreme priest, had the monopoly of legislation in church matters (*ius in sacris*). He was the supreme judicial authority, and had the supreme administrative oversight of the Roman community, which through Constantine's incorporation of the Catholic Church into the state order became a public legal body like all other Christian communities. Without asking any bishop, on his own authority Constantine convened the first ecumenical council at Nicaea and enacted church laws. Later the rumour was spread in the West that the city of Rome and the Western half of the empire were handed over to the Bishop of Rome, in the so-called 'Donation of Constantine', but this document proved to be another of history's great forgeries.

The period after AD 350 saw the slow rise of the Roman community and its bishop to a monarchical position of dominance in the West. The emperor was remote and predominantly involved in the East. He had exempted the Roman clergy from taxes and granted them their own jurisdiction over questions of faith and civil law.

Granted, the papal Rome was not built in a day. But purposefully and aware of their power, the fourth- and fifth-century bishops of Rome developed their competence in the direction of a universal primacy. The claims that they made may have had no biblical and theological foundation, but over the centuries these entered church law as accepted facts. Thus to many people today, both inside and outside the Catholic Church, what the Roman bishops of the fourth and fifth centuries attributed to themselves in a growing awareness of their power seems to be what is originally Catholic:

• Under Bishop Julius (337–52), Rome declared itself a universal court of appeal (with a questionable reference to the Western rump synod of Sardica in 343 and later with a false appeal to the Council of Nicaea).

• The unscrupulous Bishop Damasus (366–84) was the first to try to use the Matthaean saying about the rock (which he understood in a legalistic sense) to back up claims to power. He spoke exclusively of his 'apostolic seat' (*sedes apostolica*) as if there were no others. The very fine decoration of Roman tombs and churches (provided with Latin inscriptions) and the commissioning from the north Italian scholar Jerome of a better, more easily understandable, translation of the Bible (later called the 'Vulgate') were part of a cultural policy to reinforce Rome's position of power.

• Bishop Siricius (384–99) was the first to call himself 'pope'. *Papa* (from the Greek *pappas*) was a reverent, loving name for father, long used of all bishops in the East; the process of a Roman monopolization of titles originally belonging to many churches and bishops had begun. Siricius succinctly called his own statutes 'apostolic'. At the same time he adopted the style of Roman officials and the chancellery: like the emperor communicating with his provincial governors, he responded to the enquiries and requests of other churches with brief rescripts, with 'Decreta' and 'Responsa'.

• Bishop Innocent (401–17) required that after being discussed at synods, any important matter should be presented to the Bishop of Rome for his decision. With scant concern for the truth (North Africa, France and Spain are examples to the contrary), he claimed that the gospel reached the other Western provinces simply and solely from Rome; this was meant to be the basis for the imposition of a uniform liturgy.

• Finally, Bishop Boniface (418–22) attempted to forbid any

further appeal by declaring his judgements and decisions permanently binding.

However, we should note that initially all these were merely Roman claims. Especially in the East, where at first people looked down on Rome disparagingly as the old capital which had gone into decline, hardly anyone took them seriously. There, alongside the emperor, the ecumenical council, which could be convened only by the emperor, was regarded as the supreme authority.

Thus all the attempts by the Roman bishops of the fourth and fifth centuries to conclude from the biblical saying to Peter about the rock, that Roman jurisdiction over the whole church was the will of God, and to put that into practice, came to grief. And the great contemporary of Bishops Damasus, Siricius, Innocent and Boniface, the most significant theologian of the West, the North African Aurelius Augustine, who was a true friend of Rome, thought nothing of a universal legal primacy of the Bishop of Rome.

The father of Western theology

Only between 360 and 382 was Latin universally and definitively introduced in worship after a lengthy transitional period. Latin now also became the official language of the Western church, theology and law, and remained so down the centuries until, in the second half of the twentieth century, the Second Vatican Council introduced a change.

Specifically, Latin theology was grounded in North Africa: by the lawyer and lay theologian Tertullian in the second half of the second century. Already with him, what distinguishes Latin Christianity from Greek had become clear. Its main interests were not metaphysical and speculative problems of christology and the doctrine of the Trinity, but psychological, ethical and disciplinary problems: guilt, atonement, forgiveness and penitential discipline; church order, the offices and sacraments. In all this there was an emphasis on the will and a shift towards the social dimension, towards the community and the church as a political body.

All the significant bishops and theologians of the West followed the same line, especially Cyprian of Carthage, the spiritual leader of the North African church and defender of episcopal autonomy against Rome in the third century. He was followed in the fourth century by Ambrose of Milan, former prefect of the city, who like others deliberately learned from the Greek theologians: exegesis from the Alexandrian, Origen; systematic theology from the three Cappadocians, Basil, Gregory of Nazianzus and Gregory of Nyssa.

But if, towards the end of the fourth century, the Latin West was following the same theological course as the Greek East, it owed this to the life's work of a theologian who hated learning Greek but had a sovereign mastery of Latin and was to become *the* theologian of the Latin church, Aurelius Augustine (354–430). Anyone who wants to understand the Catholic Church has to understand Augustine. No figure between Paul and Luther has had a greater influence on the Catholic Church and theology than this man, who was born in present-day Algeria. Originally he was a very worldly man, an intellectual genius, a brilliant stylist and a gifted psychologist; after many wanderings and perplexities he became a passionate Catholic Christian, priest and bishop.

Augustine was Bishop of Hippo Regius (Bône in Algeria, now Annaba) for thirty-five years. As bishop, this man, who during his life wrote so much that was brilliant and profound, splendid and moving about the human longing for happiness, about time and eternity, about the human soul and devotion to God, remained an indefatigable preacher, expounder of scripture and author of theological treatises. As such, he was the main figure in the two crises which not only shook the church of Africa but would in fact decide the future church of Europe: the Donatist and the Pelagian crises.

What was the true church? Around this question revolved the first great crisis sparked off by the hard-line church of the Donatists (founded by Bishop Donatus). For decades the Donatists had been turning their back on the church of the masses, which in their eyes had become too worldly: they claimed that all baptisms and ordinations by bishops and presbyters who were unworthy, particularly those who 'fell' in persecution, were invalid, as were those of their successors.

This was disputed from the beginning in the 'great church'. Under the auspices of the state religion proclaimed by Theodosius, the Donatists were banned from worshipping; they were threatened with confiscation of their goods and banishment. Only the 'Catholic Church' was recognized by the state. In the face of the Donatist schism which was developing, Augustine, who as bishop was from the beginning intensively concerned about the unity of the church, campaigned for the universal, catholic church, which for him was the 'mother' of all believers. Already as a lay theologian he argued as follows:

> We must hold fast to the Christian religion and the fellowship of that church which is the catholic church and is named the catholic church, not only by its members but also by all its opponents. Whether they want to or not, even heretics and schismatics, if they

are not speaking among themselves but with outsiders, call only catholics catholic. For they can make themselves understood only if they give it the same name with which it is named by all the world (*De vera religione*, 7.12).

Here 'catholic church' was no longer understood as a church that embraced all and at the same time was orthodox, but now also as a church that was spread all over the earth and was numerically by far the largest. As in this case, so too in other cases Augustine provided the whole of Western theology with arguments, categories, solutions and catchy formulae, especially for a differentiated doctrine of the church and the sacraments. But because he started from a polemical and defensive position, despite his emphasis on the 'invisible church' of true believers, he developed an emphatically institutional and hierarchical understanding of the church.

So here we have the subordination of the individual to the church as an institution. Granted, Augustine understood the real church as a pilgrim church which was to leave the separation of the chaff and the wheat to the last judge. But confronted with ever new heretical groups and influenced by a crude policing action, he finally thought that even violence against heretics and schismatics could be theologically justified. He argued this by referring to Jesus's saying from the parable of the banquet, in which the Latin translation accentuates the words *Coge intrare*, 'Compel (instead of invite) those outside to come in ...' Thus down the centuries Augustine, who could speak so convincingly of the love of God and human love, indeed who defined God as 'love itself', fatally became the key witness for the theological justification of forcible conversions, the Inquisition and holy war against deviants of all kinds – something that did not occur in the same way in the Christian East.

But there were also further considerable differences between East and West.

How is salvation achieved? The second great crisis facing the church revolved around this question. This time it was sparked off by the highly regarded ascetical lay monk Pelagius, who came to Rome from England. Faced with a lax nominal Christianity among well-to-do Roman society, he attached great importance to morality, to the human will, to freedom, responsibility and practical action. God's grace – specifically the example of Jesus, moral admonition and forgiveness – was important, but for Pelagius it played more of an external role. At any rate he did not understand grace as Augustine, following Tertullian, understood it: as a 'force' (Latin *vis*) working inwardly in people, almost reified as a spiritual fuel, which in the Middle Ages would be called 'created grace' as opposed to the graciousness of God himself.

Augustine felt that Pelagianism touched on the weak spot of his experience, indeed struck at the heart of his faith. After all, through the wearisome years before his conversion he had experienced in his tie to a woman who bore him a son how weak his will was, how strong was 'fleshly' desire (*concupiscentia carnis*) culminating in sexual pleasure, and how human beings thus needed the grace of God from beginning to end for their conversion. In his intimate poetic *Confessions* he described the grace which must be given to sinful man wholly and utterly by God. Here Augustine referred in a new way to the Pauline message that sinful human beings are justified, put right with God, through grace by faith, and not by works fulfilling the law. This message had lost all topicality as a result of the disappearance of Jewish Christianity and the Greek concentration on the divinization of human beings. Indeed, he put the theme of grace at the centre of Western theology.

But the battle against the Pelagians had momentous consequences. For in the zeal of battle Augustine sharpened and narrowed down his theology of sin and grace. He now attempted to explain the sin of every human being from the biblical story of the fall of Adam, 'in whom (instead of after whose example) all human beings sin'. That is a downright mistranslation of Romans 5.12. In this way Augustine historicized, psychologized, indeed sexualized Adam's primal sin. For him, in complete contrast to Paul, it became original sin which was determined sexually. For, according to Augustine, this original sin was transmitted to every new human being through the sexual act and the 'fleshly', i.e., self-centred desire (concupiscence) connected with it. Therefore, according to this theology, every infant has already fallen victim to eternal death – unless it has been baptized.

The consequence is that Augustine, who more than any author of antiquity had a brilliant capacity for analytical self-reflection, bequeathed to the whole Catholic Church of the West the doctrine of original sin, which was unknown in the East, and at the same time a fatal vilification of sexuality, the sexual libido. Sexual pleasure for its own sake (and not for the procreation of children) was sinful and to be suppressed – to the present day this remains the baneful teaching of the Roman pope.

At the same time Augustine took over another pernicious myth from the dualistic sect of the Manichees. This sect, to which he belonged for a while in his youth, was hostile to the body, and held that only a relatively small number of human beings were predestined for bliss (to make good the gap which has come into being through the fall of the angels). The others were a 'mass of perdition'. This cruel doctrine of a double predestination (the predestination of some to bliss and the others to damnation) was at the opposite pole to Origen's teaching about a universal reconciliation to be hoped for at the end. In Western Christianity it would similarly have an insidious effect and disseminate an infinite amount of anxiety about salvation and fear of demons – down to the Reformers Luther and Calvin, who would consistently think this teaching through to the end.

The Trinity reinterpreted

For many years Augustine laboured indefatigably on a great work of his old age, prompted to it not by heresy but rather out of an inner need for clarification: he was concerned to present a deeper, more convincing reinterpretation of the doctrine of the Trinity. His interpretation would come to command such a following in the Latin West that people would hardly be aware of any other. But to the present day it is resolutely rejected by the Greeks. Why?

The Greek church fathers always began from the one God and Father, who for them, as for the New Testament, was 'the God' (ho theos). They defined the relationship of God the Father to the Son and Spirit in the light of this one God and Father. It is as if we have a star which gives its light to a second star ('light of light, God of God') and finally to a third. But to our human eye, all three stars appear one after the other only as one star.

Augustine differed completely: instead of beginning from one God and Father he began from the one nature of God, or divine substance, which was common to Father, Son and Spirit. For the Latin theologians, the principle of unity was not the Father but the one divine nature or substance. To develop the illustration given earlier: three stars do not shine one after the other but side by side in a triangle at the same level; here the first and the second stars together give light to the third.

To explain more precisely, Augustine used psychological categories in a new way: he saw a similarity between the threefold God and the three-dimensional human spirit: between the Father and the memory, between the Son and the intelligence, and between the Spirit and the will. In the light of this analogy the Trinity could be interpreted as follows:

The Son is 'begotten' from the Father 'according to the intellect'. The Father knows and begets in the Son his own word and image. But the Spirit 'proceeds' from the Father (as the lover) and the Son (as the beloved), 'according to the will'. The Spirit is the love between Father and Son become person: it has proceeded from both the Father and the Son. (It was the Latin term denoting this proceeding also from the Son, *filioque*, which proved to be the great stumbling block for the Greeks. Their view was that the Spirit proceeded only from the Father.)

Thus Augustine had made an intellectual 'construction' of the Trinity with philosophical and psychological categories in an extremely subtle way, as a self-unfolding of God. Here the 'and the Son' seemed so essential that in the West from the sixth/seventh century it was gradually inserted into the creed. Time and again it was required by the German emperors after Charlemagne, and in 1014 it was definitively inserted by Rome into the ancient creed. But even today the East still regards this *filioque* as a falsification of the old ecumenical creed and as clear heresy. However, similarly, to the present day, those Catholic and Protestant dogmatic theologians of the West who attempt to make what is claimed to be the 'central dogma' of Christianity credible to their contemporaries, with every possible modernization and new argument (usually in vain), hardly seem to be aware that they are interpreting the relationship between Father, Son and Spirit not so much in the light of the New Testament as in the light of Augustine.

The City of God

In the last period of his life Augustine became involved in a crisis of a quite different kind: a crisis in world history which did not involve the church but the Roman empire. On 28 August 410, Rome, which regarded itself as 'eternal', was stormed by the army of Alaric, the King of the West Goths, and plundered for days. Atrocity stories about the rape of women, the murder of senators, the hunting down of the rich and the destruction of the old centre of government and administration reached Africa. Defeatism was widespread: if 'eternal Rome' could fall, what was still safe? Wasn't Christianity to blame for everything? Did the whole of history still have a meaning?

Augustine reacted with a last, grandiose, dramatic work, *The City of God* (*De civitate Dei*). In it he took up every counter-argument. He did not refer in any way whatsoever to the Byzantine New Rome, which was intact, but rather developed a theodicy in the grand style through all the seven eras of the world: a justification of God in the face of all the riddles and catastrophes, which issued in a large-scale interpretation of history. What is the basis and meaning of world history? His answer is that the whole of world history is ultimately a violent battle between

– the *civitas terrena*, the earthly state, the world state, the citizenship of the world (in the background of which stands the diabolical state of the hybrid angels who have fallen from God), and

– the *civitas Dei*, the city of God, God's state, the citizenship of God.

Thus with every possible parallel, analogy, allegory and typology Augustine offered an overall view of world history which in its deepest dimension is a great clash between belief and unbelief, humility and arrogance, love and the quest for power, salvation and damnation – from the beginning of time to today and also to a final end, namely the eternal city of God, the kingdom of peace, the kingdom of God. All in all, this was the first monumental theology of history in antiquity, which was to have a wide influence down to the Middle Ages in the West, and also in the Reformation up to the threshold of the modern secularization of history.

Of course, Augustine would have felt that to glorify the Roman Church and the pope as 'God's state' (and to discredit the German emperors and their empire as the 'world's state') was a misuse of his work. He had no interest in institutions and individuals: he was far from politicizing and clericalizing God's state. The pope plays no part in 'God's state'. For Augustine, in any case, all bishops were fundamentally equal: though for him Rome was the centre of the empire and the church, he gave no boost to papalism. He did not think in any way in terms of a primacy in rule or jurisdiction for Rome. For it was not Peter as a person (or even his successor) who was the foundation of the church, but Christ and faith in him. The Bishop of Rome was not the supreme authority in the church; the supreme authority was the ecumenical council, as it was for the whole of the Christian East, and Augustine did not attribute any infallible authority even to this.

Barely two years after he had completed this 'great and extremely difficult work', *The City of God*, Augustine heard the terrible news that the Arian people of the Vandals, which in a generation had gone right through Europe, from Hungary and Silesia to Spain and Gibraltar, were now marching along the coast of Mauritania, plundering and burning. In 430 Hippo was besieged by the Vandals for three whole months. Augustine, now seventy-five years old, smitten with fever, prepared for his end with the penitential psalms of David. Before the Vandals broke through the defensive cordon, on 28 August – twenty years to the day after the conquest of Rome by the Goths – Augustine died. He was the undisputed spiritual and theological leader of North Africa, where Roman rule had now collapsed for ever. But Augustine's theology was to make world history on another continent, Europe.

Down to our day, this catholic theologian who in spite of his errors is beyond compare, recalls the meaning not only of world history but also of human life when, in the closing sentences of his *City of God*, he conjures up that indescribable and indefinable eighth day on which God completes his work of creation: 'There we shall rest and we shall see. We shall see and we shall love. We shall love and we shall praise. Behold what shall be in the end and shall not end. For what other thing is our end, but to come to that kingdom of which there is no end?'

IV   The Papal Church

The first real pope

The Catholic imperial church, which spanned the whole inhabited world, became the Western Catholic Church as we know it in a slow process lasting for centuries, between late antiquity and the early Middle Ages. Alongside the specifically Latin theology of Augustine, which provided the theological foundation, the development of the Roman papacy, which had already long been prepared for, now became important as the central institution of church rule. It formed the foundation in church politics for the new constellation or paradigm of the church that was to develop.

Leo I (440–61), a solid theologian and excellent lawyer, a zealous preacher and pastor and a capable statesman, is the one to whom historians give the title 'pope' in the real sense. This is not only because this man, who in church history is called 'the Great', was brimming over with the Roman sense of mission but because he succeeded, with theological clarity and legal acuity, in forging together the biblical, historical and legal elements prepared for in previous centuries into the classical synthesis of the Roman idea of primacy.

His argument was:

Biblical: Leo argued that a primacy of Peter over all other apostles was already grounded in the New Testament. He understood the classic passages relating to Peter in the crudely legalistic sense of a 'fullness of power' (*plenitudo potestatis*) given to Peter, a primacy of rule for the leadership of the whole church.

Historical: Leo saw the Bishop of Rome as Peter's successor substantiated in a letter from Pope Clement to James, the brother of the Lord, in Jerusalem. According to this, in a last testament Peter made Clement his sole legitimate successor. But the letter was a forgery from the end of the second century and was translated into Latin only at the end of the fourth century and the beginning of the fifth.

Legal: Leo defined the legal position of Peter's successor more precisely with the help of the Roman law of inheritance. The successor might not inherit the personal characteristics and merits of Peter, but he did inherit the official authority and function handed on by Christ, so that even an unworthy pope was a completely legitimate successor and held office as such. So the simple question was that of the office, which was assumed immediately on accepting the election, even if the person elected should still be a layman and not an ordained priest (this still holds today).

Through him, Peter spoke personally: with this high consciousness of office Leo led the Western church and could even persuade the emperor of West Rome to acknowledge his primacy. He was the first Bishop of Rome to adorn himself with the title of the pagan chief priest, *Pontifex Maximus*, which the Byzantine emperor had dropped. In 451, with a Roman delegation, he went to negotiate with Attila in Mantua and succeeded in preventing the Huns from sacking Rome. Four years later, however, he was unable to stop the capture and plunder of Rome.

In the same year, 451, Leo suffered a bitter defeat at the Council of Chalcedon, at which the crucial issue of the relationship between the divine and the human in Christ was defined: his three legates were flatly refused the precedence which they claimed. Despite his explicit prohibition, the letter which Leo had sent on the issue was first of all checked by the council to see if it met the norms of orthodoxy, and only then did his christological formula meet with approval. Not only was he not accorded any privileges over the whole church, but the church status of a city was made dependent on its civil status. Consequently the see of New Rome was given the same primacy as the old imperial capital. The protest of the Roman legates rang out unheard at this great council with its six hundred members, as did Leo's protest afterwards. But his delay of two years in recognizing the council helped only its opponents in Palestine and Egypt, from among whom the non-Chalcedonian churches emerged: the monophysite Coptic Church in Egypt, the Nestorian Church in Syria and the Armenian and Georgian Church. They still exist today.

However, in Rome people had every reason for gratitude for Leo's championship of their city: Leo was the first Bishop of Rome to be buried in St Peter's. More importantly, his successors continued to operate on the same theological and political lines. A provisional climax to the Roman claim to power was the pontificate of Gelasius I at the end of the fifth century. Completely under the rule of the Arian Theodoric, King of the Goths, the Bishop of Rome succeeded in operating largely independently of Byzantium. And supported by Augustine's doctrine of the two kingdoms, he could with impunity develop the claim to an unlimited supreme priestly authority over the whole church which was completely independent of the imperial authority. Emperor and pope had different functions in one and the same society: the emperor had only worldly authority, the pope only priestly authority. But the spiritual authority was considered superior to the worldly authority of the emperor, as it was responsible for the sacraments and, before God, also responsible for those who exercised worldly power. This doctrine developed by Leo and Gelasius, a pope later in the century, completely detached the clergy from the worldly order and jurisdiction. To this degree Walter Ullmann has called the doctrine the Magna Carta of the medieval papacy. Here the theoretical basis of the papal claim to world power was already being laid. However, as the following centuries were to show, for a long time this still remained Roman wishful thinking.

Errant popes, papal forgeries and papal trials

In the sixth century the Emperor Justinian renewed the Roman empire from Constantinople. He built Hagia Sophia, the greatest church in Christendom, and fully established the Byzantine state church, politically, legally and culturally. All heretics and pagans lost state offices, titles of honour, authority to teach and public salaries. The Second Rome, Constantinople, was not only put on the same level as the old Rome, but politically was clearly superior. The bishops of Rome again felt the emperor's primacy in law.

The Eastern patriarchs and metropolitans certainly still regarded the pope as bishop of the old imperial capital and sole patriarch of the West. But as such he was first among equals. And this was not, say, because of a special biblical 'promise' or a legal 'authority', but, as always, because of the tombs of the two chief apostles, Peter and Paul. Of course no one at that time, even in Rome, would have thought that the bishops of Rome were infallible.

In the sixth and seventh centuries decisive setbacks followed the expansion of papal power in the fourth and fifth centuries.

Above all, now, two famous cases of errant popes (which were still vigorously being discussed at the First Vatican Council in 1869–70, though finally ignored by the majority) showed the limits and fallibility of the authority of Rome.

Under Justinian, of all emperors, Pope Vigilius (537–55) presented such contradictory theological viewpoints in the face of heretical monotheism at the fifth ecumenical council held in Constantinople in 553 that he lost all credibility. Later he was not even buried in St Peter's, and down the centuries was ignored even in the West.

Pope Honorius I was even worse. At the sixth ecumenical council held in Constantinople in 681, and then also at the seventh and eighth ecumenical councils, he was condemned as a heretic; this was confirmed by his successor Leo II and by subsequent Roman popes.

Historical research, notably that of Yves Congar, has shown that down to the twelfth century, outside Rome the significance of the Roman Church was not understood as a real teaching authority in the legal sense ('magisterium') but as a religious authority, which was given with the martyrdom and tombs of Peter and Paul. No one in the whole of the first millennium regarded decisions of the pope as infallible.

But historical research has also shown that the popes, particularly from the fifth century on, decisively extended their power with explicit forgeries. The freely invented 'legend' of the holy Pope Silvester comes from the fifth/sixth centuries. In the eighth century it led to the highly influential forgery, the 'Donation of Constantine' (only shown to be a forgery in the fifteenth century), according to which Constantine left Rome and the Western half of the empire to Pope Silvester; allowed him the imperial insignia and garments (purple) and a court to match; and bestowed on him the primacy over all other churches, especially Antioch, Alexandria, Constantinople and Jerusalem. In fact, Constantine had left him only the Lateran palace and the new basilicas of the Lateran and St Peter's.

Also from the fifth/sixth centuries came the writings of the pseudo-disciple of Paul, Dionysius the Areopagite. He introduced the word 'hierarchy' and a whole hierarchical system: as in heaven (angels) so on earth (clergy). Finally, from these centuries date the equally successful forgeries from the circle around Pope Symmachus, the second successor of Gelasius, which among other things made the statement *prima sedes a nemine iudicatur*. The pope ('the first see') may not be judged by any authority, even by the emperor.

Reality, however, was completely different: the East Goth Theodoric the Great, perhaps an Arian Christian, sent Pope John I as a mediator to Constantinople, but when John's mission failed, Theodoric summarily threw him into prison, where he was to die. During Justinian's absolutist rule of forty years, he summoned the bishops of Rome to his court when necessary, and there their orthodoxy was examined. After his decree of 555 the imperial *fiat* ('Let it be done') had to be obtained for any election of a bishop of Rome; moreover, this was carried out down to the time of the Carolingians. Indeed, in the sixth and seventh centuries there was a whole series of trials of popes – elected by the emperor or by the clergy and people of Rome. These proceedings often ended with the deposition of the pope. They were to continue into the fifteenth century.

Christianity becomes Germanic

Alongside the Latin theology of Augustine and the development of the Roman papacy as a central institution of rule, there was a third element without which the Catholic Church of the Middle Ages would have been inconceivable: the Germanic peoples. These peoples in particular, largely still pagan, uncultivated but vital, without any universal perspectives, would ensure that the *ecclesia catholica* did not go under with the Roman empire.

When the Vandals, Alans and Suevi (driven on by the Huns who were moving up from the steppes of southern Russia) flooded the empire, along with the West Goths, Alamans, Burgundians and Franks, they broke up the Roman state and Roman law and also let the highly developed infrastructure, the state buildings, road systems, bridges and aqueducts, go to ruin. This was an unprecedented economic, social and cultural relapse, connected with the depopulation of the cities and a decline in the capacity to write, as in higher education generally. It was a relapse which could only be made good to some extent many centuries later. Rome, the world city, with sometimes more than a million inhabitants, had by the sixth century sunk to the level of a provincial city with only 20,000 inhabitants.

In the midst of the collapse of ancient civilization, with all its confusions, wars and destructions, the church initially withdrew in the face of the uncultivated Germanic peoples. Cities like Cologne, Mainz, Worms and Strasbourg, which had become Frankish, and also other cities from northern Gaul to the Balkans, had now had no bishop for more than a century. Only later did Christianity return: first with the East Goths in present-day Bulgaria through the activity of Bishop Ulfila, who created a Gothic script, literature and translation of the Bible;

from Bulgaria also among the West Goths; and finally among most Germanic peoples. However, everywhere this was a Christianity stamped by Arianism.

At all events, now there was a Christianizing of the German world and at the same time a Germanizing of Christianity. Under the influence of the Romans of the Western province, whose Latin now developed into the national languages (French, Italian and Spanish), that Germanic people which were to create the most important kingdom of the West, namely the Franks, became Catholic. Clovis, King of the Franks, was baptized in 498/9. The Byzantine Emperor then recognized the new power, from which just three hundred years later, to the indignation of the Byzantines, a new rival, Western 'barbarian' empire would emerge. Among the Franks, too, instead of a trained Roman officialdom the nobility took over the leading role: state possessions and money became the property of the king and the nobility, who also assumed sovereignty over the church and the right to nominate bishops.

The Catholic Church represented the decisive factor of continuity in this fundamental revolution. The rulers (whether the Goth Theodoric the Great, the Frank Charlemagne or the Saxon Otto the Great) could not read or write; only the clergy could. Only they could hand on the ancient literature and, in time, create a new written culture. This happened through the monasteries, which were now also becoming increasingly numerous in the West. Alongside the hierarchical structure of the bishops and their dioceses, as a result of the work of the Irish-Frankish monastic movement (Columban the Younger) a gigantic network of monasteries developed, more than five hundred in Gaul alone. Throughout the Middle Ages the clergy possessed and preserved the monopoly on education. But the office of bishop was also reinforced; now the bishop often received political dominion over a city, with a multiplicity of worldly tasks, so that his office became the privilege of leading families.

Medieval piety

The Christian substance was certainly preserved: the Christianized Germanic peoples, too, believed in the one God and his Son Jesus Christ and the Holy Spirit; they administered the same baptism and celebrated the same eucharist. Yet everything else, the overall constellation, changed.

• Instead of adult baptism, almost everywhere there was only the passive-unconscious baptism of infants.

• Instead of the early church's liturgy of the people, there was a liturgy of the clergy which offered a sacral drama in an incomprehensible sacral language (Latin) to the people, who looked on passively.

• Instead of the once-for-all public penance of the early church, there was now auricular confession, propagated by the Irish-Scottish monks, which could be repeated at any time and which was not yet tied to the ordained priest.

• Instead of the veneration of martyrs at their tombs, common in the early church, there was a massive veneration of saints and relics.

• Instead of highly reflective theology, there was Germanic superstition further than the eye could see, especially the intense belief in spirits which was to be found in all ethnic religions.

• Instead of education, increasing importance was attached to celibacy, not only among clergy belonging to religious orders but also among the secular clergy, although the marriage of priests was still customary. But the ordination of women as deacons, the order below priests, which was still usual in the fifth century, was now abolished – just one expression of a heightened unbiblical hostility to women which is to be found in the church.

The last of the Latin church fathers, and at the same time the first medieval pope, was Gregory the Great (590–604). Because he was simple and popular, he was often more widely read than his teacher Augustine. Critical scholarship makes, above all, his *Dialogues on the Life and Miracles of the Italian Fathers* responsible for the dissemination of crude stories of miracles, visions, prophecies, angels and demons. Gregory was also without doubt responsible for the theological sanctioning not only of a massive veneration of saints and relics but also for the idea of purgatory and of masses for souls. He was excessively interested in sacrifices, penitential ordinances, categories of sins and punishments for sins, and he put excessive emphasis on fear of the eternal judge and hope for reward for good works. After Pope Gregory, who died in 604, Latin theology was almost completely silent until Anselm of Canterbury in the eleventh century.

But even critical scholarship recognized that Gregory, the wise ascetic from a rich aristocratic family, was an able politician and lovable pastor of souls, in short, an excellent bishop of Rome. He did not become a prince of the church and a 'political pope' but at heart remained a monk and an ascetic. This bishop with practical concerns was in control of his administrative apparatus, and toiled extremely effectively to ensure that the papal estates from North Africa and Sicily to Gaul were of benefit to the population of Rome, which was often in want. No wonder that in the confusions of war he took on increasing responsibility for administration, finance and the welfare of the people and that he thus imperceptibly laid a basis for the secular power of the papacy. But this man, who always understood himself to be the chief 'servant of the servants of God' (*servus servorum Dei*), was always concerned above all with the spiritual good of the church. Therefore Gregory encouraged monasticism, and through his account of the life of Benedict, the founder of the monasteries of Subiaco and Monte Cassino, known only in a shadowy way, made Benedict the model abbot and father of monks. Moreover, the Benedictine order combined old monastic traditions with the military spirit of Rome. It had a rule which, in view of the numerous itinerant ascetics, committed members to *stabilitas loci*, i.e., to remain in one place; to obedience to the abbot; to the renunciation of property and marriage; and to manual work (from agriculture and crafts to copying manuscripts, both ancient and Christian). For the secular clergy, Pope Gregory's *Regula pastoralis* (*Pastoral Rule*) presented the ideal pastor of souls. Gregory also took great care over cultural work, for example in connection with the Lateran library, and over liturgical singing. However, the notion that he invented 'Gregorian chant' is a legend.

'Rule from the highest place is good if the one who is in charge is more in control of his vices than of his brothers.' That was a characteristic saying of Pope Gregory from his *Pastoral Rule* (II, VI, 22). Whereas Leo the Great advocated a proud and dominating understanding of primacy, Gregory the Great advocated a humble and collegial one. Had the papacy of the subsequent period orientated itself more on Gregory than on Leo in its understanding of office, the *ecclesia catholica* of the Middle Ages could have developed along the lines of the earliest church and the early church could have become a Catholic *communio* with a democratic collegial constitution, and with a Roman primacy of service. But the papacy in the following period orientated itself more on Pope Leo and attempted to build up a hierarchical church with an authoritarian and monarchical constitution after the example of the Roman emperors, with a Roman primacy of rule. However, a papal *imperium Romanum* inevitably led to further alienation and finally resulted in the split between the church of the West and the church of the East. For the ambitions of Rome, and the theological and legal justifications for a sole dominion, understandably did not appeal to anyone in the Christian East, where emperor and council still had supreme authority.

Islam

Pope Gregory the Great, who since his activity as a legate in Constantinople had had no illusions about the difficulty of carrying through a Roman primacy of jurisdiction in the East, was the first pope to recognize the latent creative powers of the Germanic peoples and extended his sphere of action northwards and westwards: to France, to the Spanish kingdom of the West Goths, and especially to Britain, a land which became one of those most loyal to the pope. The English historian Edward Gibbon is said to have remarked that Caesar used six legions to conquer Britain, Gregory only forty monks. In contrast to the two churches already in existence – the old British church and the Irish monastic church – Gregory's missionaries brought a Christian faith with a marked Roman stamp, which the Irish/Scottish and Anglo-Saxon monks of the sixth to eighth centuries would also preach in Germany and in Central Europe. To this extent Pope Gregory laid the foundations for the spiritual and cultural unity of 'Europe'. But it was a Europe made up of the south, west and north – without Greece and the East.

However, in the same seventh century in the East a completely new opponent of Christianity began its unprecedented victorious course, namely Islam. For Christianity, the expansion of Islam meant a catastrophe on a grand scale. In North Africa Christianity disappeared almost completely – apart from the Egyptian Copts. The great churches of Tertullian, Cyprian and Augustine went under. The patriarchates of Alexandria, Antioch and Jerusalem sank into insignificance. In short, the lands in which Christianity originated (Palestine, Syria, Egypt and North Africa) were subsequently lost (the conquests during the Crusades were only an interlude). The excessive complications of the dogmas of christology and the Trinity, and the inner divisions of Christianity by comparison with the simplicity of the Islamic confession of faith (the one God and his prophet) and the initial cohesion of Islam, essentially contributed to the downfall.

The result of the victorious course of Islam was a shift in the focal point of world politics. Through the loss of its southern and south-eastern territories, the empire of East Rome seemed decisively weakened by comparison with the West. At the same time the unity of the Mediterranean ecumene of the early church was broken for ever. The kingdom of the Franks now had the opportunity to form a new *Imperium Christianum*; to this degree, as Henri Pirenne remarked, Muhammad first made Charlemagne possible. For Christianity, in geographical terms this meant a shift of focus not only westwards, but also to northern Central Europe – with completely new possibilities for Rome, in particular.

A state for the pope

Now the Catholic Church was left as the only cultural force in the West, the heir to the education and organization of late antiquity. It alone – under the leadership of the papacy and with the help of monasticism, above all the Benedictine order – was capable of shaping over the long term the culture, morality and religion of the Germanic and Romance peoples, who in many respects were primitive. The leading figure in building up the dioceses among the Germanic people was the Anglo-Saxon monk Boniface (really Wilfrid), who was consecrated archbishop in Rome and as papal vicar for the whole of Germania prepared for papal rule in the kingdom of the Franks. Thus for many centuries, as a matter of course, the Catholic Church remained the institution which dominated the whole of cultural life.

But at that time no Western universal church had yet formed. For in the Germanic churches, which were tribal churches, regional churches or the ruler's 'own' churches, it was not the pope but the king and the nobility who had the say. That also applied to the kingdom of the Franks, which was rising in the eighth century and, after the conquest of the Spanish kingdom of the West Goths by the Arabs, became the only kingdom on the continent of Western Europe between the Pyrenees and the Elbe.

The papacy shrewdly went along with developments and brought about a momentous turning-point in world politics: it broke with the Byzantine emperor (who in any case was paralysed by the iconoclastic dispute between those who revered icons and those who wanted to abolish them in Orthodoxy) and allied itself with the Frankish ruling house – in the hope of a state of its own. And, after a century, that in fact came about. However, the royal major-domo Charles 'Martel' (a military 'hammer'), who safeguarded the Frankish heartland in battle against the Arabs at Tours in 732, refused to intervene against the Langobards of upper Italy who were threatening Rome. But his son Pippin, who was planning a *coup d'état* against the decadent Merovingian shadow kings, needed higher legitimation because of his lack of 'royal blood'. Only the pope could give him this, and moreover the pope boldly appointed himself kingmaker: he had Pippin anointed king with holy oil as in the 'Old Testament', possibly by Archbishop Boniface. This laid the foundation for the Christian notion that the king in the West could only be 'by the grace of God', i.e. the pope.

Pippin showed his gratitude. In two campaigns he conquered the Langobard empire and gave its territories in northern and central Italy to 'holy Peter', the pope. However, in the view of Rome, where the 'Donation of Constantine' had been forged fifty years earlier, this Donation of Pippin was only giving 'back' to the pope what had belonged to him since Constantine. Be this as it may, after the theological and ideological foundation, now the economic and political foundation had been laid for a church state which was to last over eleven centuries, to the year 1870.

The second great blow against Byzantium was struck by Pippin's son Charles. On the pretext of a vacancy on the throne (in Byzantium a woman, Irene, was ruler), on Christmas Day 800, in St Peter's, for the first time Pope Leo III took upon himself the right to crown the emperor: Charlemagne, who did not see himself only as emperor of the West, was crowned by the pope autonomously with his own valuable crown as 'Emperor of the Romans' (and thus also of the East). What a provocation for Byzantium! For, all at once, there were now two Christian emperors, and in the West the Germanic emperor was increasingly regarded as the true and only legitimate one, because he had been 'anointed' with holy oil by the pope himself.

The Western equation: Christian = Catholic = Roman

In connection with the new empire, in the West the ecumenically pernicious equation Christian = Catholic = Roman increasingly became established. This laid the foundation not for the unity but for the division of Europe. Even in Charlemagne's universal empire, which now stretched from Schleswig-Holstein far beyond Rome and from the Ebro to the Elbe, there was still no corresponding universal papal church. Even in the West there was still no trace of a papal primacy in law, but there was a primacy in law of the emperor.

For Emperor Charlemagne, lord of the empire, felt quite theocratically that he was also lord of the church. Imperial politics was church politics and church politics was imperial politics. Moreover, without any moral or religious scruples, Charlemagne also imposed his form of Christianity on his subject peoples and did not shrink from costly and cruel wars: in the case of the Saxons these lasted for thirty years, with thousands of people executed or deported. The 'unity of the empire' came first for him. The Franks regarded the pope as the guardian of the apostolic traditions, responsible for questions of faith and the liturgy, but restricted to purely spiritual functions.

Charlemagne was so fascinated by the myth of Rome (empire, language, culture) that in his imperial palace in Aachen he ushered in a 'renaissance' of ancient literature with an international team of capable scholars. At the same time he was active as a zealous reformer of the church who concentrated quite specifically on the duties of the bishops, on the establishment of parishes and communities of canons in the cathedrals, and on the participation of all the faithful in worship.

But however much Charlemagne required that all Christians should know the Lord's Prayer and the creed in their mother tongue, he wanted the official liturgy to be celebrated in Latin. In the interests of the empire he had the Roman liturgy transplanted into the Frankish kingdom. For the first time in church history a liturgy was celebrated in a foreign language, Latin, understood only by the clergy, instead of in the vernacular – a situation which was to last until the Reformation and indeed in the Roman Catholic Church until the eve of the Second Vatican Council.

Here it was not the simple Roman parish liturgy which was adopted in the kingdom of the Franks but the highly ceremonial papal liturgy: combined with that, there was a tremendous increase in genuflections, signs of the cross and the use of incense. On the other hand, there was now a 'silent mass' celebrated by the priest alone without the people, whispered since it was no longer understood. In more and more cathedrals there were more and more individual masses at more and more individual altars. Altar and congregation were alienated; the priest stood with his back to the people. And as no one could formulate prayers spontaneously in Latin any longer, everything was now written down and prescribed to the last word: a liturgy of the book. The communal eucharist was hardly still celebrated as such (later, participation once a year had to be prescribed). It was replaced by the 'typically Catholic mass', in which the activity of the people was completely limited to looking on, to watching the sacral drama of the clergy.

Catholic morality

From the Middle Ages onwards, Catholic morality was essentially the morality of the confessional. Private confession, which could be repeated without limitation, and which came not from Rome but from the Celtic monastic church, spread amazingly quickly throughout Europe. Public penance before the bishop, characteristic of the early church, no longer played a role; any priest could give private absolution. Already at the time of Charlemagne it was said that the eucharist could not be received without confession of sins, an important reason why the eucharist was received only very rarely.

In setting penances, the priests usually went by the penitential books – attributed to the Irish saints Patrick and Columban – which determined the level of punishment. There would be no confession and absolution of sins without satisfaction. But after the ninth century penances were increasingly postponed to after confession and absolution, and eventually could even be replaced by payments of money; this inevitably led to social injustices and countless abuses.

In the penitential books, attention was paid above all to the sexual sins. This was understandable at a time when – beginning with Charlemagne and his numerous concubines – sexual immorality was rampant. But Augustine's negative evaluation of sexuality had meanwhile established itself completely in medieval penitential morality: original sin was transferred by the sexual pleasure of the marital act. A rigid approach to sexual morality was adopted on a broad front. Sexual continence was required of the clergy, and of the laity no contact with the holy figures. Male semen, like blood at menstruation and in giving birth, caused ritual uncleanness and excluded those involved from receiving the sacraments. But married people were also to abstain from sexual intercourse on every Sunday and on all high feast-days together with the evening before, the vigil, and the eighth day afterwards, the octave, and on certain weekdays (Fridays), and in Advent and Lent. Thus there was a rigorous restriction of marital sexual intercourse which in part went back to widespread archaic, magical notions.

But now, at any rate, a typically medieval piety had taken hold, which with its prayers, sacraments and customs visibly embraced the whole of human life from the cradle to the grave, from early in the morning until late in the evening. It was constantly activated not only on Sundays but also on feast-days, which were becoming increasingly numerous. But it is worth noting that all the early medieval developments, welcome or unwelcome, and especially the Carolingian innovations and changes – liturgy restricted to the clergy and the sacrifice of the mass, private masses and mass stipends, episcopal power and priestly celibacy, auricular confession and monastic oaths, monasteries and the piety of All Souls, the invocation of the saints and the veneration of relics, exorcisms and blessings, litanies and pilgrimages – were not constants but variables of Christianity, medieval variables, which were now increasingly controlled, shaped and developed along Roman lines.

The legal basis for future Romanization

Charlemagne's empire could not be held together, and with his sons it collapsed into three important groups of countries (through the Treaty of Verdun in 843): France, Italy and Germany. However, the Roman Catholic framework was preserved. And precisely at the time of the downfall of the Carolingians in the middle of the ninth century there was a further major forgery which, once again, decisively reinforced the ecclesiastical power of the Roman papacy.

A century before the foundation of the church state a pope by the name of Nicholas I came to power who in full 'Petrine' consciousness of his office for the first time dared to proclaim an anathema (exclusion from the church) on anyone who failed to observe a papal decision regarding doctrine or practice. With the utmost boldness he attempted to suppress the self-administration of the national churches, which had previously been customary, in favour of a central Roman authority. He treated arrogantly not only bishops, archbishops and patriarchs but also kings and emperors, as if they were his to command. He unexpectedly threatened the king of the Franks with excommunication simply because of a difficult marriage situation and summarily deposed the powerful archbishops of Cologne and Trier because they supported the king.

This particular pope now – in good faith? – adopted not only the Donation of Constantine but also those far more monstrous forgeries which had been prepared in the kingdom of the Franks by a whole group of highly expert forgers, probably clergy, in order to attribute them to an Isidorus Mercator, otherwise unknown. These were the famous/notorious pseudo-Isidorean Decretals, which in the edition disseminated contained more than seven hundred closely printed sides. There were 115 completely forged documents by Roman bishops from the first centuries, and 125 authentic documents falsified by later interpolations and changes. For what purpose? Intrinsically to strengthen the position of bishops in the face of powerful archbishops. But how? The forgeries gave the impression that the early church had been ruled by papal decrees down to the details of its life. So who benefited? In fact, this was not so much to the benefit of the bishops as to that of the pope, who was designated 'head of the whole earth' and whose authority was heightened in an unparalleled way by these forgeries. To be specific: the right previously exercised by the king to hold and confirm synods was attributed solely to the pope; accused bishops could appeal to the pope; in general, all 'serious matters' were kept for the pope to make a final decision on. Indeed, state laws which contradicted the canons and decrees of the pope were regarded as void.

Pseudo-Isidore's official work of reference was soon disseminated throughout Western Europe, and only at the time of the Reformation did the anti-Roman historians who produced the 'Magdeburg Centuries' demonstrate the inauthenticity of the Decretals. The papal chancellery would have been quite capable of detecting forgeries. Why did it do this only when it was in its own interests? It never bothered to investigate the major forgeries which spoke in its favour, even when, at the end of the first millennium, Emperor Otto III for the first time declared the time-honoured Donation of Constantine to be a forgery.

Almost all of these forgeries from the ninth century gave the impression that papal claims which were made only from the middle of the fifth century onwards were time-honoured and the will of God. They provided theological and legal legitimation to claims to power which had previously lacked this. Now the image of the church and church law was wholly concentrated on the authority of Rome. The forgeries of Symmachus prepared the way for the Donation of Constantine, and both were taken up and consummated in this third and greatest forgery, that of Pseudo-Isidore. Together these three forgeries formed the legal basis for a future total Romanization of the Western church and the simultaneous excommunication of the Eastern church, which was now no longer reckoned to be part of 'Europe'.

All these forgeries are not curiosities 'of the time', as papal historians well-disposed towards the pope want to make out, but have had an abiding impact on the history of the church. The forgeries, most of which were subsequently 'legitimized' by the pope, still appear in the *Codex Iuris Canonici* revised under the supervision of the Curia and promulgated in 1983 by John Paul II. Anyone who so wishes can discover that this medieval curial system of power cannot claim to be based on the New Testament and the common tradition of the Christianity of the first millennium. It rests on ever new appropriations of power down the centuries and on forgeries which gave them legal legitimation. Thus, for example, according to the *Codex Iuris Canonici* which was valid up to the Second Vatican Council, the legal principle, which is important down to our day, that the pope alone can legitimately summon an ecumenical council (and that if he did not want to, no one could object), is based on five proof texts from earlier legal sources, three from the forgeries of Pseudo-Isidore and the others derived from these forgeries. But in the ninth century none were the wiser.

V   *The Church is Split*

A revolution from above

Even the forgeries of Pseudo-Isidore and the power-hungry machinations of Nicholas I still by no means brought about a total victory for the curial system. Nicholas had weak and in some ways corrupt successors; indeed, the tenth century is regarded in the historiography of the church as the *saeculum obscurum*, the dark century. It was a period of constant intrigues and battles, of murders and acts of violence, of popes and anti-popes. One need only think of the macabre exhumation of Pope Formosus after nine months, so that a judgement could be passed on his dead body. His body was sentenced, the finger of his right hand with which he gave the blessing was chopped off, and his corpse was finally thrown into the Tiber. Or one might think of the rule of terror of the 'senatoress' Marosia who, as tradition has it, was the mistress of one pope (Sergius III), murderess of a second (John X) and mother of a third (her illegitimate son John XI). She held her son prisoner in Castel San Angelo until, on her third marriage, she was imprisoned by her stepson Alberich, who then ruled Rome for two decades as 'Dux et Senator Romanorum'. The popes of this time were his powerless instruments.

The Augustinian distinction between 'objective' office and 'subjective' holder, who could also be quite unworthy, allowed the papal institution as such to survive. But the popes could not pull themselves out of the mire by their own bootstraps. It took the kings of the East Frankish empire to rescue the papacy, first of all the Saxon Otto the Great who, fascinated by his model, Charlemagne, deposed the immoral John XII, elected pope at the age of sixteen, and had elected as his successor a layman, Leo VIII, who was then consecrated to all the orders in a day, a procedure which in theory would still be legitimate even now. But the depositions and institutions of popes, popes and anti-popes, murdering and murdered popes, continued apace.

Finally, an effective reform of the papacy came about, initiated by French monasticism, implemented by the German monarchy and finally completed by the papacy itself. The papacy was fundamentally reorganized in three historical stages:

1. The Burgundian monastery of Cluny became the cradle of a monastic reform orientated on Rome in accordance with old Benedictine ideals: the monastery was freed from the supervision of the local bishops and put under the direct supervision of the pope. This 'exemption' was introduced contrary to a decree of the Council of Nicaea and justified by an alleged papal 'privilege'. In return, the monasteries had to send an annual 'census' to Rome. This provided considerable income for the papacy and at the same time spread a dense network of very well endowed points of support throughout Europe.

2. When political intrigues had led to three rival and corrupt popes drawn from the Roman nobility reigning simultaneously, at synods held at Sutri and Rome in 1046, the German king Henry III had all three deposed. He then nominated Bishop Suidger of Bamberg, who according to tradition was elected pope by the clergy and people of Rome. Clement II, as he became, was followed by a series of good imperial and mostly German popes. But these were the very ones who unintentionally built up the papacy, which was to prove the emperor's greatest enemy.

3. Under Pope Leo IX from Lothringia (1049–54), a relative of King Henry III, leadership in the reform movement passed over to the pope himself. In five hectic years Leo reformed the Roman urban clergy, and made the 'cardinals' (*cardines*, 'hinges', representatives of the Roman city churches) a kind of papal senate. He also appointed to this body highly intelligent and highly motivated representatives of reform from beyond the Alps, above all Humbert of Lothringia, now Cardinal Bishop of Silva Candida, a learned and wily theoretician of an absolutist papal rule, and then, initially in a subordinate position, Hildebrand, the archdeacon who often represented the Pope as a travelling legate. For the first time, through journeys in Italy, France and Germany a pope made effective public appearances at assemblies of clergy and synods.

It was this Humbert of Silva Candida, as the closest confidant of the pope, a skilled stylist, often ironic and sarcastic, a lawyer and theologian, who presented a whole programme for church policy in a number of publications and put it into practice in countless papal letters and bulls. Humbert was the shrewd champion of the Roman principle, which was the basis for the Roman system that soon took shape: the papacy was the source and norm of all law, its supreme authority, which could judge all but could not itself be judged by any. The pope was for the church what the hinges are for the door, the foundation for the house, the source for the river, the mother for the family. And this church was related to the state as the sun is to the moon or the soul to the body or the head to the members.

Such effective doctrines and images represented an offensive, a campaign for a new world order, albeit one that had very little to do with the constitution of the church in the New Testament and the church of the first millennium. Specifically, the Roman agitation concentrated on two points: on the battle against 'investiture' (appointment to office) by a layman, and the battle against the traditional marriage of priests, which was denigrated as 'concubinage'.

All in all this was a bold revolution from above, presented by its Roman advocates – with the aid of the forgeries – as a restoration of the order of the early church, one that was also to apply to the East. It is not surprising, then, that Humbert, this programme-maker who believed in the pope and an unbounded propagandist of the Roman principle, was also the cardinal legate who in 1054 brought about that fateful break with the church of Constantinople which has proved impossible to heal down to the present day.

The split between the church of the East and the church of the West was prepared for over long centuries by a progressive alienation. It was increasingly driven on by a gradual development of papal authority, which for Eastern Christianity was in complete contradiction with its own tradition, that of the early church.

Of course many other factors played a role in this process of alienation: different languages (the Roman popes no longer knew Greek and the ecumenical patriarchs knew no Latin), different cultures (the Greeks appeared arrogant, pedantic and devious to the Latins, the Latins uneducated and barbarous to the Greeks), different rites (liturgical, ceremonial, indeed the whole form of life and faith in theology, piety, church law and organization). Moreover, the Greeks did their bit in alienating themselves everywhere they were in power by forcing Greek on non-Greeks.

But these cultural and religious differences need in no way have led to a split. Rather, ecclesiastical and political factors were responsible for this, primarily the threatening growth of papal power. To the present day, for the Orthodox Church, the church of the 'seven councils' from the First Council of Nicaea in 325 to the Second Council of Nicaea in 787, the papal claim to primacy is the only serious obstacle to the restoration of church communion. We should remember that for the East, 'church' has primarily remained *koinonia, communio*: a 'fellowship' of believers, of local churches and their bishops, a federation of churches with a collegial order, which is based on common sacraments, liturgical orders and confessions of faith. It is the opposite of a uniform church, understood above all in legal terms, monarchical, absolutist and centralist, predominantly based on Roman church law and on Roman decrees which were completely unknown in the East. In short, such a pope-centred uniform church was an unacceptable innovation for the whole of the East. People there had never asked for papal Decreta and Responsa, had never asked for a papal 'exemption' to be bestowed on monasteries, had never had bishops nominated by the pope forced on them, had never recognized an absolute and direct authority of the Bishop of Rome over all bishops and believers.

But Rome attempted indefatigably, with all the means of its canon law, its politics and its theology, to cover up the old church constitution and to establish the Roman legal primacy of all churches in the East as well, setting up a centralistic church constitution which was wholly tailored to Rome and the pope. The consequence was a reciprocal alienation of the churches, in three main phases. As we have seen:

• In the confusion of the barbarian invasions in the fourth/fifth centuries, the Roman bishops did all they could to fill the power vacuum in the West with their own power. Popes Leo I and Gelasius attempted to establish the principle of the *papal church* – an unlimited supreme priestly authority over the whole church, quite independent of imperial power – as opposed to the *imperial* church.

• In the seventh/eighth centuries Pope Stephen travelled to the King of the Franks to be guaranteed a church state at the expense of former Byzantine territories. Then Pope Leo III promised on his own authority to Charlemagne the title of Caesar, which was previously reserved for the Emperor of Byzantium, and thus alongside the only legitimate emperor crowned a new, Western, Germanic emperor by the grace of the pope. Finally the haughty Nicholas I excommunicated the Byzantine Patriarch Photius, a respected theologian and a bishop accustomed to thinking in pastoral terms, and who came to be venerated in the East as a saint. Photius defended the traditional patriarchal autonomy of East Rome and also opposed the introduction of a *filioque*, declaring that the Holy Spirit proceeds from the Son as well as the Father, into the traditional creed of the councils.

• And now, in the eleventh/twelfth centuries, the arrogant and theologically prejudiced Humbert met the theologically uneducated and equally arrogant Patriarch Cerularius. Immediately on arrival Humbert denied Cerularius the title of Ecumenical Patriarch, openly doubted the validity of his ordination, and agitated quite publicly against him. Indeed, finally, on 16 July 1054, he placed a Bull of excommunication against the 'bishop' of Constantinople and his helpers on the altar of Hagia Sophia, thereupon to be excommunicated himself by the patriarch along with his escort.

Since then, the break between the church of the East and the church of the West has proved irreparable, despite all the attempts at reconciliation. The split would be sealed by the Crusades, which began towards the end of the eleventh century. By them, Rome hoped not only to force back Islam, but finally to bring the unbiddable 'schismatic' church of Byzantium under papal supremacy. For by now popes had attained to a fullness of power with which they could feel themselves masters not only of the church, but also of the world.

A Romanized Catholic Church

It had taken around six hundred years for the papacy, after countless setbacks and defeats, to shape a *Roman* Catholic Church, for which the foundations were laid by Augustine and the Roman bishops in the fifth century, and in so doing to realize the programme developed by Leo I and Gelasius. The aim of this programme was sole rule by the pope in the church and the world, allegedly established by the apostle Peter, indeed by Jesus Christ. The church was now Roman through and through. The Roman Church was to be understood as 'mother' (*mater*) and 'head' (*caput*) of all the churches, and to her obedience was due. A Roman mysticism of obedience, which in part persists in the Catholic Church to the present day, had its foundation here: obedience to God must be obedience to the church, and obedience to the church obedience to the pope.

And why not? Now in Rome there was a wealth of documents and decretals and an effective publicity machine to implement, step by step, the primacy of papal rule supported by history and dogma, shaped in law and with a developed organization. Leo IX's successor would be the last pope to be nominated by a German king. And his successor in turn, Nicholas II, would be the first pope to have himself crowned, like kings and emperors. He declared the college of cardinals the exclusive organ for electing the pope (the clergy and people of Rome might only confirm the election) and appointed it as an advisory organ ('consistory') to the pope.

At this point there appeared on the world stage the man who had already played a key role behind the scenes as papal legate, the Archdeacon Hildebrand. While the funeral ceremonies for Nicholas II were still going on, he was elected tumultuously, with a crass failure to observe the requirements for papal elections. He called himself Gregory VII (1073–85). Hard as a diamond and a man of passionate convictions (his fellow cardinal Peter Damian called him a 'holy Satan'), he radically and irrevocably instituted what would be called the 'Gregorian reform' and became involved in the historic 'investiture dispute' with the German king and emperor Henry IV.

For Gregory VII, all legal prerogatives followed quite logically from the 'fullness of power' (Leo I, *plenitudo potestatis*) given by God to Peter's successor. Gregory declared the pope to be sole and unrestricted ruler of the church, set over all believers, clergy and bishops, churches and councils; supreme lord of the world, to whom even all rulers and the emperor were subject, as they too were 'sinful human beings'; and indubitably holy on taking office (by virtue of the merits of Peter); after all, the Roman Church, founded by God alone, has never erred and never can err.

Thus an unlimited competence in matters of consecration, legislation, administration and judgement was claimed for the pope. In 1077, a good twenty years after the break with the East, this stance inevitably led to the historic conflict with the German king and emperor, the most important ruler in Europe, Henry IV. Contrary to all the laws of the early church, in his fanatical battle against the marriage of priests Gregory VII declared all priestly activities of married priests invalid; indeed, he called on the laity to revolt against their priests. He renewed, in a very strict form, the prohibition against the widespread practice of the lay investiture of clergy and sent serious warnings to the young Henry IV. Henry, however, had no intention of ceasing to appoint bishops. The issue was, who was the supreme authority within Christendom, king or pope? Then Gregory threatened excommunication. Henry, badly advised, reacted at the Reichstag by deposing the pope, but he could not enforce this act at a distance and it had little credibility in the new situation, which in view of the publicity of Humbert and others had changed in favour of the pope.

Gregory shocked the world by excommunicating and deposing the king, suspending all the bishops who supported him and freeing subjects from their oath of allegiance. In the end King Henry capitulated. Left in the lurch by his bishops and princes, he travelled over the Alps in the bitterly cold winter of 1077, with his young wife, his two-year-old son and his court, and came to stand barefoot and in the garb of a penitent in front of the castle of Canossa at the foot of the Apennines. There he asked the pope for forgiveness. At first Gregory was unmoved, but after a three-day penance by Henry and on the pleading of Mathilde, the mistress of the castle and the Arch-abbot of Cluny, the pope reinstated Henry.

But Gregory's triumph at Canossa was short-lived, and the remainder of his reign was marked by failure. The election of an anti-king led to a civil war in Germany; the second excommunication of Henry fell flat. Rome was besieged by Henry, and an anti-pope was enthroned. Gregory had to flee to Castel San Angelo and was finally liberated by the Normans; however, his 'liberators' plundered and burned Rome for three days. So Gregory and his Normans had to retreat to southern Italy. There in Salerno he died in 1085, abandoned by almost all the world. His last words were: 'I have loved righteousness and hated iniquity, therefore I die in exile.'

What Gregory VII had fought for, suffered for and in the end only achieved to a limited degree, his secular and imperial ambitions for the pontificate, were most fully realized during the reign of Innocent III (1198–1216), perhaps the most brilliant pope ever to rule. In him, claim and reality coincided completely. Elected pope at the age of thirty-seven, this shrewd lawyer, capable administrator and refined diplomat, who was also a theological writer and skilled orator, was a born ruler. Beyond dispute he represented the climax, but also the turning-point, of the medieval papacy.

The Fourth Lateran Council of 1215 convened by Innocent, with around two thousand bishops, abbots and plenipotentiaries of secular rulers, was a pure papal synod, which demonstrated the power of the papacy as much as it showed how insignificant the episcopate was in practice. It was no longer the emperor, as at the ecumenical councils of the first millennium, but the pope who convened the council, presided over it and confirmed the seventy decrees which had been well prepared by his Curia. However, they largely remained mere paper, apart from a papal tax on the whole clergy, compulsory confession and communion at Easter, and the resolutions against the Jews, which in many respects anticipated later anti-Semitic measures: the Jews were to wear special dress to isolate them, were prohibited from holding public office or going out on Good Friday, and had to pay a compulsory tax to the local Christian clergy. As already under Gregory VII, so too under Innocent III, papalism and anti-Judaism went hand in hand.

Under Innocent III Romanization reached its climax, and five overlapping processes were consolidated into the hallmarks of the Roman system which remain to the present day: centralization, legalization, politicization, militarization and clericalization.

(i) *Centralization*. The absolutist papal church declared itself mother. In the early church and the Byzantine church, the church was still understood as a fellowship (*koinonia*, *communio*) with no centralistic authority over all churches. By contrast, the Catholic Church of the West after Gregory VII and Innocent III presented itself as a church which in faith, laws, discipline and organization was completely orientated on the pope. Here was a fixation on an absolute monarch who, as sole ruler, had supremacy in the church. This no longer had anything at all to do with the original New Testament models of the church.

Innocent III preferred the title 'Representative of Christ' (*vicarius Christi*) to that of 'Representative of Peter', which had been used for every bishop or priest down to the twelfth century, and as pope saw himself set between God and humankind. For him, the apostle Peter (the pope) was the 'father' and the Roman Church the 'mother' (*mater*). 'Mother' was now used, as required, both for the universal church as the mother of all believers and also for the Roman Church as the mother, the 'head' (*caput*) and 'mistress' (*magistra*) of all other churches. Indeed, the universal church was virtually identified with the Roman Church. This claimed to be 'Mother and Head of All Churches of the City (*urbis*) and the Earth (*orbis*)', as can still be read today in large letters on the Lateran basilica.

(ii) *Legalization*. The church, governed by law, needed a science of church law. From the beginning, the early church and the Byzantine church were legally incorporated into the imperial state and remained so. By contrast, from the Middle Ages onwards, the Catholic Church of the West developed a church law of its own, with its own science of canon law. In complexity and sophistication this was equal to the state law, but it was now totally centred on the pope, the absolute ruler, legislator and judge of Christianity, to whom even the emperor was subordinate.

The time of the Gregorian reform saw the origin in Rome of professional collections of law in the Roman spirit. The popes of the twelfth century promulgated more legal decisions for the whole church than all their predecessors put together. Because there were so many of these, too many to comprehend, and they were so uncertain and contradictory, at that time there was a universal welcome for a summary textbook produced by Gratian, the Camaldolese monk teaching at the University of Bologna, the *Decretum Gratiani*. (However, 324 passages from popes from the first four centuries were taken from the Decretals of Pseudo-Isidore, and of these 313 were demonstrably forgeries.) No wonder that the professional 'canonists', 'church lawyers', in fact 'papal lawyers', became an inestimable ideological support for the Roman system in Rome, as in countless chancelleries and courts of Europe.

On the basis of the *Decretum Gratiani*, in time three official collections of papal decrees, and an unofficial one, were made. Together, these formed the *Corpus Iuris Canonici*, on which the *Codex Iuris Canonici* of 1917/18 was based. Only with this legal learning did the papal monarchy have the instruments and personnel for putting the Roman claims into practice in the everyday life of all the churches. Of course there was no trace of a division of authorities: the pope was at the same time the supreme leader, absolute lawgiver and supreme judge of the church, to whom one could appeal in all things. However, even under Innocent, these appeals were the cause of the worst abuses, including trade in legal privileges; they were arbitrary, partisan and up for sale.

(iii) *Politicization*. This powerful church claimed to dominate the world. In the early church and the Byzantine church, the power of the church was bound up with a system of 'symphony' and harmony, a partnership in which the secular power in fact dominated the spiritual power. By contrast, from the Middle Ages on, through the papacy the church of the West presented itself as a completely independent ruling body of the first rank, which sometimes also managed to gain almost complete control of the secular power.

As 'sinful men', in the papal view emperors and kings were subordinate to the pope: in coming centuries, too, the popes would constantly intervene in worldly affairs, indirectly or directly. However, in the investiture dispute a compromise had to be agreed on. The election of bishops now took place through the clergy and nobility of the diocese, and from the thirteenth century through the cathedral chapter, though this would hardly elect a bishop who was unacceptable to Rome. Unlike Gregory VII, who had no sense of proportion, Innocent combined boldness and resolution with a statesmanlike wisdom and tactical flexibility. By a skilful anti-German policy of 'recuperation' ('repossession'), he became the second founder of the church state (which was now almost twice the size). In Innocent's time Rome was indisputably the predominant and busiest centre of European politics. Indeed, Innocent really did rule over the world, if we understand that not as absolute dominance but in terms of being the supreme arbiter and the greatest liege lord.

(iv) *Militarization*. A militant church waged 'holy wars'. The Orthodox churches of the East, too, were entangled in most of the political and military conflicts of the Byzantine empire and often gave theological legitimation to wars, even inspired them. But only in Western Christianity was there that (Augustinian) theory of the legitimate use of violence to achieve spiritual ends which finally also allowed the use of violence in the expansion of Christianity. Contrary to the tradition of the early church, there were wars of conversion, wars against pagans, wars against heretics; indeed, in a complete perversion of the cross, there were Crusades, even against fellow Christians.

Already with Gregory VII we have a pope intensely preoccupied with a plan for a great campaign in the East. Gregory personally wanted to lead a great army as general in order to establish Rome's primacy in Byzantium and end the schism. As champion of 'holy war', he sent the 'banner of Peter' ('the blessing of Peter') to those parties in a war whom he favoured and thus blessed their cause. And as early as ten years after the death of Gregory, Urban II summoned the First Crusade, a holy war under the sign of the victorious cross. The Crusades were regarded as an affair of the whole of Western Christianity, said to be approved by Christ himself. For the pope had personally issued the summons to them as Christ's spokesman. As the Crusades usually took men over thousands of miles and often through enemy territory, without any basic provisions and under indescribable strain, they would not have been possible without real religious enthusiasm, passion, and often almost mass psychosis.

With hindsight, Innocent III's policy of crusades was tragically misguided. With the initiation of the Fourth Crusade (1202–4), which led to the fateful conquest and three-day plunder of Constantinople, to the erection of a Latin empire with a Latin church organization, and to the enslaving of the Byzantine church, the papal goal – the establishment of the Roman primacy in Constantinople – at last seemed to have been achieved. However, the opposite was the case: the rape of Constantinople in fact sealed the schism.

This pope also proclaimed a first great crusade against Christians in the West at the Fourth Lateran Council in 1215, against the Albigensians ('neo-Manichaean' Cathars) in the south of

France. The cruel Albigensian war, which lasted for twenty years, marked by bestial cruelties on both sides, led to the extermination of whole sections of the population and represented a shaming of the cross and a perversion of what was Christian. It is no wonder that around this time, among protest groups of an evangelical character, the notion began to spread that the pope was the Antichrist and, increasingly, the question was asked whether the Jesus of the Sermon on the Mount, the man who proclaimed non-violence and love of one's enemy, would ever have approved of such a warlike undertaking. Was not the cross of the Nazarene being perverted into its opposite if, instead of inspiring the real bearing of the cross every day by Christians, it legitimated bloody wars waged by Crusaders wearing the cross on their garments?

(v) *Clericalization*. A church of celibate men established the prohibition of marriage. In the Eastern churches the clergy, other than the bishops, remained married and were therefore much more integrated into the structure of society. By contrast the celibate clergy of the West were totally set apart from the Christian people, above all by their unmarried state: they had a distinctively prominent social status which, because of its higher moral 'perfection', was in principle superior to the lay state and was totally subordinate only to the Roman pope. Moreover, the pope was now for the first time supported by an omnipresent celibate auxiliary force with a central organization, prepared and mobile: the mendicant orders.

Under the influence of the monks Humbert and Hildebrand, in a kind of 'pan-monasticism', Rome required of the whole clergy unconditional obedience, the renunciation of marriage and a common life. Gregory VII took the extraordinary step of calling on all the laity of Christendom to boycott the ministries of married clergy. There were revolting witch-hunts of priests'

99

wives in the clergy houses. After the Second Lateran Council of 1139, priestly marriages were regarded as *a priori* invalid and all priests' wives as concubines; indeed, priests' children officially became the church's property as slaves. There was furious mass protest by the clergy, especially in northern Italy and Germany, but to no avail. Henceforth there was a universal and compulsory law of celibacy, though in practice up to the time of the Reformation this was observed only with qualifications, even in Rome.

More than anything else the medieval law of celibacy contributed to the separation of the 'clergy', the 'hierarchy', 'the priestly state' from the 'people', who were the 'laity', and completely subordinate to the clergy. In terms of the balance of power, this meant that the laity were in fact excluded from the church; the clergy alone, as the stewards of the means of grace, formed 'the church', and this clerical church with its hierarchical, monarchical organization culminated in the papacy.

Under Innocent III, the second branch of the clergy, the clergy in religious orders, became increasingly important. For the pope shrewdly domesticated the growing poverty movement in the church and approved those novel orders whose animating principle was the discipleship of the poor Jesus: the mendicant orders, the begging orders, of the Franciscans and Dominicans.

Despite all his successes, the triumphal pontificate of Innocent III proved to be the apex of the pope's temporal power. More than this pope could suspect, he undermined the love of the people for the seat of St Peter by his power politics, enforced with spiritual compulsion, with ban and interdict, and with guile, deception and oppression. Already under Innocent, those terrifying manifestations of decline became evident which were to form the main accusations of the Reformers, and which in part have remained marks of the curial system down to our day. There was nepotism and the favouring of the pope's relatives, along with the officials and the cardinals, greed, corruption, the 'excusing' and concealment of crimes, and the financial exploitation of the churches and peoples by a cleverly devised system of offerings and taxes. All those taking part in the Fourth Lateran Council had to give a 'parting present' to Innocent, who was always devising new sources of revenue.

From a political perspective, the papacy of the high Middle Ages could list considerable gains: lay investiture had finally been abolished; the German empire had seen its power to impose its will gutted; within the Latin church the papacy had totally established itself as the institution whose power to rule was absolute, in complete contrast to the traditional episcopacy and the synodical structures of the early church. The independence of the church from the state, and the autonomy of the clerical sphere from the other spheres of life, had also been realized. Indeed, through its legal system the papacy had become Europe's central institution.

However, these gains were accompanied by considerable losses – tribulations both external and internal. The more time went on, the more the Crusades proved a fiasco. Islam remained Christianity's greatest opponent, and at the same time, the absolutist papacy permanently lost the churches of the East with the excommunication of the patriarch, the Fourth Crusade and the establishment of a Latin empire in Constantinople (which proved to be only transitory). And through the destruction of the universal German empire the papacy also undermined its own position as a universal Roman papacy. Unintentionally, it provided a powerful impetus for the formation of modern nation-states, and its anti-German policy at the same time made it openly dependent on France, which increasingly played host to the papacy in times of political turmoil. At the same time, at first imperceptibly, this became a great threat to the papacy itself.

Heretics and the Inquisition

After the 1170s and 1180s, two great nonconformist movements focused on penitence and poverty developed and posed a threat to the Roman system – an organized opposition within the church. In the face of a Christianity which church law had made rigid, rich monasteries, and a senior clergy who lived in luxury and neglected the duty to preach, these movements took as their programme the slogans 'lay preaching' and 'apostolic poverty'.

First of all came the Cathars (from the Greek *katharoi* = 'the pure', hence also the German word *Ketzer*, 'heretic'). They spread from the Balkans, around the middle of the twelfth century, through itinerant preaching in the manner of the apostles and strict asceticism: abstention from eating meat, from marriage, from military service, from oaths, from altars, and from saints, images and relics. Also called Albigensians, after one of their centres, the city of Albi in the south of France, the Cathars increasingly advocated a doctrine with a Manichaean structure which spoke of a good and an evil principle and formed a real counter-church with its own hierarchy and dogma, a church made up of 'believers' and the 'perfect', marked out by their asceticism.

Then there were the Waldensians, a product of the West, who emerged from an ascetic lay brotherhood centred on the rich merchant Waldo from Lyons: converted to the Sermon on the Mount on the basis of a Provençal translation of the Bible, Waldo distributed his wealth among the poor. Again there was a dispute with the hierarchy over lay preaching. Many people became radicals because they were excluded from the church. A distinctive lay church came into being with its own liturgy, administration of the sacraments, lay eucharist and lay preaching (by men and women alike). Like the Cathars, Waldensians rejected oaths, military service, altars, church buildings, the veneration of the cross, the idea of purgatory, and the death penalty.

What was the response of the official church, first the bishops, then the pope, with the full support of the emperor? As a rule, it answered initially with the prohibition of lay preaching and the condemnation of the 'heretics'. But excommunication and the use of the legislation applying to heretics only drove these religious movements underground and made them even better known – as far as Bohemia, where later the Hussites and the Bohemian Brethren adopted some of the Cathars' teachings.

Aroused by a zeal to eradicate the 'heretical' threats, bishops and popes, kings and emperors, prepared what would fill many of the most terrible pages of church history under the dreaded name of the Inquisition – the systematic legal persecution of heretics by a church court (*inquisitio haereticae pravitatis*) which enjoyed the support not only of the secular power but also of broad groups among the people, who often eagerly looked forward to the execution of heretics. The Inquisition would become an essential characteristic of the Roman Catholic Church.

One decisive influence on the development of the Inquisition was the Emperor Frederick II, who in his coronation edicts stipulated death at the stake as the punishment for heresy. Another was Pope Gregory IX, nephew of Innocent III, who by means of a constitution took upon himself the whole fight against heretics, which was previously organized mainly by local bishops. He nominated papal inquisitors, above all from the mobile mendicant orders, to track down heretics. This universal papal Inquisition served to relieve, expand and intensify the episcopal inquisition, which had its roots in the early Middle Ages.

Heretics condemned by the church were to be handed over to secular judgement – for a fiery death or at least to have their tongues cut out. As for the laity, they were not to discuss the faith either privately or publicly, but were to denounce all those who were suspected of heresy. Church authorities alone could decide on matters of faith, and no freedom of thought and speech was allowed. Innocent IV in particular, a great lawyer pope, went one step further. He authorized the Inquisition also to allow torture by secular authorities in order to extract confessions. The physical torments this caused for the victims of the Inquisition beggars any description.

Only the Enlightenment would remove the barbarisms of torture and the stake for heretics, but the Roman Inquisition would continue under a different name ('Holy Office', 'Congregation for the Doctrine of Faith'), and even today its proceedings accord with medieval principles. The proceedings against someone who is suspected or accused are secret. No one knows who the informants are. There is no cross-examination of witnesses nor are there any experts. The proceedings are kept closed, so that any knowledge of the preliminaries is prevented. Accusers and judges are identical. Any appeal to an independent court is ruled out, or is useless, for the aim of the proceedings is not to discover the truth but to bring about unconditional submission to Roman doctrine, which is always identical with the truth. In short, the goal is 'obedience' to 'the church', in accordance with the formula which is still in use: *humiliter se subiecit*, 'he has humbly submitted'. There is no question that such an Inquisition mocks both the gospel and the generally accepted sense of justice today, which has found expression in particular in the declarations on human rights.

In a very important case, however, we owe it to a change in Innocent III's policy about heretics that some individuals and groups were not excluded as heretical, but remained incorporated into the church: this is the case of the evangelical and apostolic movement of the so-called mendicant orders, based on poverty. Whereas Innocent had stubborn, intractable heretics like the Cathars exterminated with fire and sword, he gave the new movements founded by Dominic and Francis of Assisi a chance of survival within the church.

As early as 1209, six years before the Fourth Lateran Council, a truly historic meeting took place between Francis of Assisi and Innocent III, the *poverello*, the little poor man, and the sole ruler. The great alternative to the Roman system took shape here in the person of Giovanni di Bernardone, the name given at birth to the happy-go-lucky worldly son of a rich textile merchant from Assisi.

Innocent III was already aware of the urgent need for reforms of the church, for which he would soon convene the council. He was sensitive enough to observe that the outwardly powerful church was inwardly weak, that the 'heretical' currents in the church had increased powerfully and that it was difficult to overcome them solely with force. Would it not be better to bind them to the church and meet their wish to engage in apostolic preaching in poverty? In principle, Francis of Assisi was not unwelcome to him.

But precisely what was the concern of the *poverello*? What was the meaning of the 'rebuilding of the fallen church' which the twenty-four-year-old understood to be his calling in a vision of the crucified Christ in 1206? It was nothing less than an end to a self-satisfied bourgeois existence and a beginning of real discipleship of Christ in poverty and itinerant preaching in accord with the gospel, indeed conformity to the life and suffering of Christ and identification with Christ (*alter Christus* = 'a second Christ'). Specifically, the Franciscan ideal has three key points:

(i) *Paupertas*, poverty: a life with absolutely no possessions, not only for the individual member of the brotherhood (as in the earlier orders) but also for the community as a whole. Money, church buildings and the quest for Roman privileges were prohibited. The brothers were to work hard in the fields; they were to beg only in an emergency. So Francis did not want a mendicant order.

(ii) *Humilitas*, humility: a life which renounced power and influence to the point of extreme forms of self-denial and mortification, patience in all situations, and a basic mood of joy which could endure even taunts, shaming and blows.

(iii) *Simplicitas*, simplicity: discipleship of Christ in great simplicity in all that was done. Knowledge and learning were nothing but obstacles here. Instead, there was to be a new relationship to creation, as was expressed above all in the 'Hymn to the Sun': a new relationship to animals, plants and inanimate phenomena of nature; all living creatures were brothers and sisters.

In conformity with Jesus, but not in confrontation with the hierarchy, not by drifting into heresy but in obedience to pope and Curia, Francis and his eleven lesser brothers (*fratres minores*) were to realize their purpose and, like the disciples of Jesus, proclaim the ideal of the gospel life everywhere through itinerant preaching. On the basis of a dream according to which, as the tradition goes, a small, inconspicuous religious prevents the papal basilica of the Lateran from collapsing, the pope finally approved Francis's simple rule and published it in the consistory. But nothing was fixed in writing.

However, all this also meant that Francis, dangerous though he seemed, had committed himself wholly to the church. He had promised obedience and reverence to the pope and bound the brothers by the same promise. At the wish of his patron, Cardinal Giovanni di San Paulo, he even had himself and his eleven companions elevated to the clerical state by the tonsure. This made their preaching activity easier, but at the same time furthered the clericalization of the young community. Priests too now joined the society. The process of the 'ecclesiasticization' of the Franciscan movement had begun, and Francis, who had wanted to detach himself from all things in poverty, was now all the more dependent on 'holy mother church'. Behind this stood above all the nephew of Innocent III, Cardinal Hugolino, who during Francis's lifetime made himself his friend and protector. A year after Francis's death Hugolino ascended the papal throne as Gregory IX, canonized Francis, against Francis's express wishes had a splendid basilica and a monastery built in Assisi, and relaxed the Franciscan rule by adding constant interpretative qualifications. At the same time, as we have seen, he established the central Roman Inquisition.

Francis of Assisi, with his gospel demands, was originally the alternative to the centralized, legalistic, politicized, militarized and clericalized Roman system. It hardly bears thinking about: what would have happened had Innocent III, instead of integrating Francis into this system, taken the gospel seriously and adopted the key points of Francis of Assisi? What would have happened had the Fourth Lateran Council introduced a reform of the church on the basis of the gospel?

Innocent III died unexpectedly, seven months after the conclusion of the council. On the evening of 16 June 1216 he was found in the cathedral of Perugia, abandoned by all, completely naked, robbed by his own servants. He was probably the only pope who, on the basis of his unusual qualities, could have shown the church a fundamentally different way, who could have spared the papacy a split, and exile, and the church the Protestant Reformation. Even if a great church cannot be so enthusiastic and idealistic that it ignores the complicated questions of the exercising of office and the law; in other words, even if offices must be handed on in a legitimate way, the law must be implemented and financial transactions carried out; the basic question still remains: Should the Catholic Church be a church in the spirit of Innocent III or in the spirit of Francis of Assisi? We recall the key words of Francis's programme:

• *Poverty*: Innocent III stood for a church of wealth and splendour, of greed and financial scandal. But would not also a church have been possible which had a transparent financial policy, was content and made no claims, was an example of inner freedom from possessions and Christian generosity, and did not suppress the life of the gospel and apostolic freedom but furthered them?

• *Humility*: Innocent III stood for a church of power and rule, of bureaucracy and discrimination, of repression and the Inquisition. Would not also a church have been conceivable which was modest, friendly and engaged in dialogue, was made up of brothers and sisters and was hospitable even to those who did not conform, whose leaders engaged in unpretentious service and showed social solidarity, and which did not exclude from the church new religious forces and ideas, but made fruitful use of them?

• *Simplicity*: Innocent III stood for a church whose dogma was excessively complex, for moralistic casuistry and legal safeguards, a church with a canon law which ruled everything, a scholasticism which knew everything, and a 'magisterium' which was afraid of the new. But would not also a church have been possible which was a church of good news and joy, a theology orientated on the simple gospel, which listened to people instead of merely indoctrinating them from above, not just an 'official church' which only teaches, but a people's church which keeps on learning afresh?

The great theological synthesis

Alongside emperor and pope, the Middle Ages also saw the universities take shape as a social force. In the thirteenth century these replaced the monasteries as centres of learning. They were the third great force from which, ultimately, a really new paradigm of Christianity would emerge, dominated by neither emperor nor pope.

The brilliant Thomas Aquinas (1225-74), a simple Dominican and professor of theology all his life, uninterested in church offices (he could have been Abbot of Monte Cassino or Archbishop of Naples), was perfectly situated to develop a new overall theological view. A pupil in Paris of Albertus Magnus, the naturalist and expert on Aristotle, virtually from his youth up Thomas grappled with the pagan philosopher Aristotle. Aristotle was regarded as dangerous and troublesome, and the popes – in vain – attempted to issue bans on reading his works; but not least the commentaries of Arab and Jewish philosophy, which had progressed much further than Christian theology, were making him increasingly known.

The Augustinianism which had previously governed all thought was in crisis. It was no longer possible to appeal solely to the previous authorities – the Bible, church fathers, councils and popes. Much more use needed to be made of reason and conceptual analysis. The new university theology of Albertus Magnus and Thomas Aquinas, influenced by Aristotle (unlike the Franciscan Bonaventura, later to be made cardinal, who was oriented more towards Augustine), took a decisive turn towards the creaturely and empirical, towards rational analysis and scientific research.

It was Thomas Aquinas who, above all in the *Summa contra Gentiles* and the *Summa Theologiae*, worked out a new theological synthesis by distinguishing consistently between two different modes of knowledge (reason versus faith), levels of knowledge (natural versus revealed truths) and sciences (philosophy versus theology). This was to some degree a hierarchy in which faith remained superior to reason. In this way Thomas created the mature, classical formulation of medieval Catholic theology. Initially condemned by traditionalists, it was to find recognition only much later. It brought about a restructuring of all theology by the revaluation, not only of reason as opposed to faith generally, but also of the literal meaning of scripture as opposed to the allegorical-spiritual meaning, nature as opposed to grace, natural law as opposed to Christian morality, philosophy as opposed to theology, and the *humanum* as opposed to the distinctively Christian.

Thomas Aquinas created a grandiose and novel theological synthesis, yet, although he lacked neither the knowledge nor the acuteness of intellect nor the courage, he could not produce a really new constellation of theology and the church. He was no Luther. Rather, in his 'top storey', his theological superstructure, he remained all too tied to Augustine's problematical interpretations of the truths of faith, the doctrines of the Trinity and original sin, christology, grace, the church and the sacraments. He brought Augustine's theology very much up to date, refined it and modified it with the help of Aristotelian concepts, but he did not criticize it directly and eventually replace it. Are the 'natural' truths of reason as 'evident' as Thomas assumed and, conversely, are the 'supernatural' truths of faith as 'mysterious' as he seemed to claim in his attempts to protect them against reason?

Thomas was also a great supporter of the pope. Unlike Origen, who was critical of hierarchy, and also unlike Augustine, who thought episcopally, Thomas proved to be a major apologist for the centralist papacy, and has been effectively used as such down to the present day. In this he is very much in the spirit of Gregory VII and Innocent III. Certainly in his commentary on Aristotle's *Politics* he again emphasized the value of the state alongside the church; but the papal primacy of rule still stood at the centre of his understanding of the church: his picture of the church was utterly derived from the papacy. In his work commissioned by the pope for the negotiations with the Orthodox Church with a view to reunion (*Against the Errors of the Greeks*) – unknown to Thomas, it drew heavily on the forgeries of Pseudo-Isidore and others – he could not indicate clearly enough that this 'first and greatest of all bishops', the Bishop of Rome, 'possessed the pre-eminence over the whole church of Christ' and 'in the church the fullness of authority'. In making the fatal statement 'that to be subject to the Roman pope is necessary for salvation', Thomas is in one sentence excluding the whole of the Eastern church from salvation.

Recently Thomas Aquinas has been criticized even more for not only failing to diminish Augustine's *scorn for women* but for actually heightening it. Under the influence of Aristotle in particular, he saw the male as the sole active 'procreating' part because of his sperm and the female as the exclusively receptive, passive part (the existence of the female ovum was not demonstrated until 1827). So he described woman as 'defective and failed', indeed as fortuitously a defective, 'failed man' (mas occasionatus). He also spoke out against the ordination of women to the priesthood. However, out of fairness it should be added that often Thomas was expressing only what was generally thought at the time. But fortunately the Middle Ages was not constituted solely of the elements of papacy and empire, university and theology.

The ongoing life of Christians

At this point in this short history of the Catholic Church we would do well to remember that the history of the establishment of the church as an institution, as a political power, is one thing, and the history of the authentic life of Christians is another. There is a great deal that could be said about the active charitable work of countless Christians and their concern for the suffering and the poor; about the care of the sick, which was organized at a very early stage, out of which emerged the many hospitals which still flourish to this day; about the concern for peace in the face of blood vengeance and feuds ('the peace of God' for all holy times); and the many varied and colourful lives, private and public; also the *ars moriendi*, the art and culture of dying, set against the background of endless famines, epidemics, pestilences and wars.

One would also have to take in the blossoming of chivalry, the Minnesingers and the popular epic, the incomparable Romanesque and Gothic cathedrals and their sculptures and stained-glass windows; the habits, rites of piety and intimate experiences of the laity, and the particular experiences of women – princesses, nuns and madonnas. However much Christian life was dominated by the church 'from above' in a quite practical and concrete way, acoustically by the sound of the bells and optically by the church towers which rose above all else, how could the normal Christians of the age, 'down there', who could hardly read or write, and who had little authentic news, be interested in the great battles between emperor and pope, in all the decrees and polemical writings? The power and supremacy of the local bishop was much nearer, and often cause for rebellion on the part of citizens who had grown self-confident.

Of course, faced with the sometimes cheerful and sometimes oppressive medieval piety of salvation through good works, the great festivals and colourful services, the countless processions and penitential practices, one can ask: What was really Christian about all this and what was not? What was simply custom and what was inner conviction? What was only contemporary façade and what was truly Christian substance?

And yet, indisputably in the Middle Ages, so often branded as 'dark', the essential Christian substance was retained: the same gospel, the same initiation rite (baptism), the same communal celebration (the eucharist) and the same ethic (discipleship of Christ) – despite all the overlaying, shifting, obscuring and falsification. In the Middle Ages in particular, the discipleship of Christ was certainly misunderstood: the discipleship of the cross was confused with a cult of the crucifix or with mystic immersion in the burgeoning participation in the suffering of Christ. And yet there were countless medieval men and women who unpretentiously wanted to live as authentic disciples of Jesus in everyday life: committed to their fellow men and women, especially to the weak and marginalized, the hungry, strangers, the sick and those in prison. There was an everyday practice of love of neighbour: in the Middle Ages countless people lived out their Christianity in a quite practical and natural way. This is the history of Christianity which is not listed in any church chronicles or handed down in the books of theologians.

However, one thing must be conceded. In the officious church ideal view the medieval world was a world dominated by priests, monks, nuns and their ideal of continence. These groups not only had a monopoly on reading and writing but also occupied the highest ranks in the hierarchy of Christians, because being unmarried and having no (private) possessions they alone on earth already embodied the kingdom of heaven. For those who were married, this meant that precisely because the body was now regarded as a sacrosanct temple, if it was joined to the body of the other sex at all, that could only be for the purpose of procreating children. Contraception was put on the same level as abortion and the exposure of children to die – an attitude that lingers among some Catholics even today.

Women could play a significant role as mistresses of the house, and many noblewomen exercised considerable political influence even in widowhood, but there is no escaping the fact that even in the high Middle Ages, the structure of society was utterly patriarchal. Women in the Middle Ages who were free, and not serfs, could for the most part neither offer allegiance nor swear oaths before a court. In the realm of the house and family, the will of the lord of the house ruled. Certainly the larger cities offered women more possibilities of professional advancement than before in crafts and trade, on both a small and a large scale, but they offered them neither equal rights nor the same rewards nor involvement in politics.

Through its theology and practice of marriage, the church contributed greatly to the revaluation of women in society. An indication of willingness on both sides, the consensus of both partners, was now an essential part of a marriage. But on the other hand there was an increased patriarchalization of the structures of power and norms, and in part also a legal repression of women. Church law prescribed the subject status of the woman under the man with arguments from natural law.

For the church, the nun was the ideal woman. Women remained excluded from all church offices, and because of the attractiveness of the Cathars and Waldensians, who were well disposed towards women, even preaching was forbidden. But through the monastery, in the sphere of the church, room to breathe and possibilities for action were offered to unmarried women and widows which were not offered by society. Indeed the church made a fulfilled existence possible, with rich possibilities of education and a new feminine self-confidence. A few nuns like Hildegard of Bingen, Birgitta of Sweden, Catherine of Siena and later Teresa of Avila were even active in church politics – in fact they attained an unprecedented charismatic authority.

Women played a special role in Christian mysticism, indigenous strains of which emerged in the late Middle Ages in Italy, the Low Countries, England, Spain, France and Germany. Alongside Hildegard of Bingen we find Gertrud and Mechthild of Hackeborn, Gertrud of Helfta and Mechthild of Magdeburg, though their significance was often suppressed by men like Meister Eckhart, Johann Tauler, Heinrich Seuse and Jan van Ruysbroeck. This mysticism, of men and women, represented a reaction to the increasing secularization of the church in the late Middle Ages, the transformation of theology into an academic discipline and the externalization of piety. Mysticism, which seeks salvation within, appeared to many people to be a spiritual alternative: because of its tendency towards internalization and spiritualization; its inner freedom by comparison with institutions, works of piety and the compulsions of dogma; its overcoming of dogmatism, formalism and authoritarianism in a direct intuitive experience of union with the divine presence, fellowship and unity with God.

It is not surprising, then, that the official church regarded mysticism with mistrust, indeed that the Inquisition took action against Meister Eckhart, John of the Cross and Teresa of Avila, and that the mystic Marguerite Porete ended up at the stake. Even communities of women living a worldly life, like the 'virgins and widows devoted to God' who at first in the Netherlands struggled to make a living with craftwork and charitable activity, were dubbed heretics. These 'Beguines' (probably a corruption of 'Albigensis', i.e., heretic) were suppressed by the Council of Vienne (1311) along with the parallel male societies, the Begards. Mysticism was kept on the periphery of the church, unable to exercise any significant formative influence on theology or practice.

It should be added briefly that the veneration of Mary, the mother of Jesus, which first developed in the Hellenistic Byzantine sphere (Council of Ephesus, 431: 'mother of God' instead of simply 'mother of Christ') took hold in the West in the second half of the first millennium. It reached a climax in the eleventh and twelfth centuries, above all under the influence of the Cistercian monk Bernard of Clairvaux. Now, above all, the emphasis was on the cosmic role of Mary as virgin mother and queen of heaven. This was an idealization, just as papalism, Marianism and the clerical monastic ideology of celibacy reinforced one another. On the other hand, it is easy to understand why, given the abstract realms into which christology had now been developed, the lovable human figure of Mary the woman, as in the form of the 'Madonna with the cloak', was extremely popular, in particular as the helper of the little

people – the oppressed and the marginalized. The New Testament 'Ave Maria' was now, along with the 'Our Father', the
most widespread form of prayer in the Middle Ages, soon supplemented with 'in the hour of our death'.

And it was indeed not Marianism but papalism which caused
a schism between the Western and Eastern churches, just as it
was not Marianism but papalism which would later split the
Western church.

VI *Reform, Reformation or Counter-Reformation?*

The end of papal domination

Who, at the beginning of the thirteenth century, at the time when Innocent III ruled the world, could have imagined the impotence of the papacy at the end of the same century? Here was truly a dramatic reversal. Boniface VIII (1294–1303) liked to display himself as lord of the world with great pomp, with a tiara or crown. In his first important Bull *Clericis laicos infestos* ('The laity hostile to the clergy') he declared the direction of the clergy the sole right of the pope, disputed royal jurisdiction over the clergy and threatened France and England with excommunication. In 1300 he pompously staged the first 'Holy Year' with a jubilee of indulgences providing a rich income for the Curia, which was swallowing up an increasing amount of money. The following year he provoked a conflict with the French king Philip IV, 'The Fair', and then, in the Bull *Unam Sanctam*, proclaimed the most succinct formulation of Roman teaching about the superiority of spiritual power, with Thomas Aquinas defining obedience to the pope as 'utterly necessary for salvation for every human creature'. And now, in the style of Gregory VII, this shrewd lawyer and unprincipled man of power, who suffered from something like papal megalomania, on 8 September 1303 planned the excommunication of the French king and the release of his subjects from their oath of loyalty. But times had changed since Canossa: Boniface VIII was simply arrested and imprisoned in his castle at Anagni by armed representatives of the French king and the Colonna family.

Even though the pope was subsequently freed by the people of Anagni, after his monstrous humiliation he was a broken man, and a month later he died in Rome. His successor but one, previously Archbishop of Bordeaux, was not enthroned in Rome but in Lyons, and eventually established his seat in Avignon. What people in Rome called the 'Babylonian captivity' of the popes there would last around seventy years. The next popes were all French and politically largely dependent on the French crown.

This process was more than a geographical shift of balance. The hierocratic papacy, whose moral credibility had been shaken because of its megalomaniac power politics, proved to be what Walter Ullmann has called a 'declining system' by comparison with which the nation-states that were then forming appeared as the 'rising system' of rule and justice. And, paradoxically, in the next decades the papacy was dominated by that very land which it had favoured for so many decades at the expense of the German Empire: France, which now experienced its rise to European predominance.

But anyone who thought that the popes would learn something from history and rein back their exaggerated claims was very much mistaken. The apparatus of papal officials, the financial administration and the vast mechanics of papal ceremonial were built up in Avignon at great expense. The papal state, which had been laid low, the giant new papal palace in Avignon, with its 'capella' for palace worship, and finally the acquisition of the county of Avignon required money, lots of money. The papal taxation screw on the whole of Europe was increasingly tightened: there was unparalleled exploitation of the whole church, which was lamented everywhere and which resulted in a dangerous alienation between the papacy and many countries, a bill that one day would come due.

In the late Middle Ages, the Roman papacy increasingly lost its religious and moral leadership and instead became the first great financial power of Europe. The popes claimed a spiritual basis for their worldly demands, of course, but they collected revenues with every means at their disposal, including excommunication and bans.

Not surprisingly, opposition to the pope increased tremendously in the fourteenth century. It had its basis in the universities, colleges, schools, the rising middle class in the cities and among influential literary figures and publicists. In his *Divine Comedy*, Dante Alighieri condemned Boniface VIII to hell and in his political confession *De monarchia* (written around 1310) questioned whether the papacy could exercise any worldly rule (until 1908 his work was on the papal Index of forbidden books). Even more influential was the polemical work *Defensor pacis* (1324), the first unclerical theory of the state, by Marsilius of Padua, formerly Rector of the University of Paris. He called for the independence of state authority from the church, of the bishops from the pope and of the community from the hierarchy. This 'defender of the peace' saw the main cause of the disturbances in society in the papal 'fullness of power', *plenitudo potestatis*, which lacked any biblical and theological basis. This 'fullness of power' was similarly criticized by the highly influential English philosopher and theologian William of Ockham, the head of the new nominalist theology, which went against tradition by asserting that what were thought of as universals had no separate existence but were in fact names (Latin *nomina*) of human origin. Because of the Inquisition William had fled from Avignon to Munich and was working in Germany.

Remarkably, this time saw the creation of the doctrine of papal infallibility, which is not to be found in the *Decretum Gratiani*, in Thomas Aquinas or in the words of the canonist popes of the twelfth and thirteenth centuries. It was propagated by an eccentric Franciscan by the name of Petrus Olivi, who had been accused of heresy because of his association with the apocalyptic views of Joachim of Fiore. The assertion of papal infallibility was to bind all subsequent popes once and for all to the decree by Pope Nicholas III in favour of the Franciscan order. But this early doctrine of the infallibility and irreformability of papal decision, at first not taken particularly seriously, was finally condemned in a Bull of John XXII in 1324 as the work of the devil, the 'father of all lies', to be warmed up again only by the conservative publicists and popes of the nineteenth century.

Thwarted reform

In the fourteenth century, the situation in Italy was becoming increasingly chaotic. Only in 1377 did Pope Gregory XI – on the urging of Catherine of Siena and Birgitta of Sweden, and certainly for political considerations – move his seat back to Rome, but he died the following year. His legally elected successor Urban VI began, almost immediately after his election, to show such an excess of incompetence, megalomania and outright mental disturbance that even under the traditional canonical view there was reason for an automatic dismissal from office. That same year some chose another pope, Clement VII from Geneva; but Urban VI, in Rome, had no intention of surrendering his office and after the defeat of Clement VII's troops before Rome Clement took his seat in Avignon again.

Now suddenly there were two popes in Christendom, who quickly excommunicated each other. So was born the great schism in the West, the church's second break, after that with the East. It would last four decades. France, Aragon, Sardinia, Sicily, Naples, Scotland and some territories in western and southern Germany were 'obedient' to Avignon; the German empire, central and northern Italy, Flanders and England, and the eastern and northern countries, were 'obedient' to Rome. There were now two colleges of cardinals, two Curias and two financial systems which duplicated the papal mis-economy – resulting in countless conflicts of conscience for individual Christians.

In this depressing situation, towards the end of the fourteenth century, 'the reform of the church, head and members' became the great programmatic saying throughout Europe. The reform movement was led by the University of Paris, which in the Middle Ages held something like a *magisterium ordinarium* in the church, though without claiming infallibility. Pierre d'Ailly, the chancellor of the university, and Jean Gerson provided a theological and legal basis for the *via concilii*: only a general council could help to restore the unity of the church and carry through the reform. This council may not, however, be understood, like the medieval papal councils, as an emanation of the papal 'fullness of authority'; it was a representation of all Christendom. As Brian Tierney has pointed out, this conciliar theory – later often discredited by the members of the Curia as 'conciliarism' – had its roots not in Marsilius and Ockham but in the utterly orthodox official canon law of the twelfth and thirteenth centuries, indeed in the patristic tradition of the ecumenical council as the representation of the church.

But what was to be done in the face of the two popes, neither of whom was willing to step down? In 1409, the cardinals on both sides held a general council in Pisa. There they deposed both popes and elected a new one. But neither of the old popes resigned, so the Catholic Church now had *three* popes. The 'accursed papal binity' had become an 'accursed papal trinity'.

It was the ecumenical Council of Constance, lasting from 1414 to 1418, the only ecumenical council to be held north of the Alps, which restored church unity (*causa unionis*) and took up the reform of the church (*causa reformationis*). Outside Rome there was an almost universal conviction that the council, and not the pope, was in principle the supreme organ of the church. In its famous decree *Haec sancta*, this view, which had already been held in the early church, was defined in solemn form by the Council of Constance: the council stood above the pope. As the general council, legitimately assembled in the Holy Spirit, which represented the whole church, it had its authority directly from Christ, and all, including the pope, had to obey it in matters of faith, the removal of schism and the reform of the church. Anyone who refused obedience was to be punished accordingly. There was no question of papal approval of these conciliar decrees, as was customary in papal synods, since the Council of Constance did not derive its authority from the pope but from Christ.

The severe defeat of the Roman curial system, which had led the church of the West to the verge of disaster, seemed to be sealed. The three rival popes were compelled to resign. And by a further decree (*Frequens*) the Council of Constance decreed the frequent holding of general councils to be the best means of a lasting reform of the church. The next council was to be held after only five years, the one after that seven years later, and the following councils at ten-year intervals.

Only because the moderate representatives of the conciliar idea agreed to the publication of the reform decrees did the radicals assent to the election of the new pope. However, a cardinal of the Curia, Martin V, was elected. The legitimacy of all popes since then has depended on the legitimacy of the Council of Constance and its decrees, which were of course highly inconvenient for a papalist, Rome-centred theology, since time and again there was a desire for a new council to reform the church, head and members. Roman theology prefers to quote the condemnations at Constance (*causa fidei*) of the Oxford scholar John Wycliffe and the Prague confessor John Hus. The shameful burning of the Bohemian patriot and Reformer John Hus was a scandal, when he had been promised immunity from arrest when attending the council. And the ruling that the laity were not to drink the wine at the eucharist was one of those wrong decisions which made theologians like Luther doubt the infallibility even of general councils.

But just as happened centuries later, after the hopes of Vatican II, so too after the successful reform Council of Constance there was an amazingly rapid restoration of the sole rule of the pope. The reform of the church and its constitution, which was needed so urgently, was thwarted by every possible means. Granted, there were the later councils of Pavia, Siena and Basel, but the reform was undermined: already at that time the Curia as the regulating body and permanent authority was stronger than the extraordinary institution of the council. Its slogan was: 'Councils come and councils go, but the Roman Curia remains.'

Still, even at that time the reinforcement of papal absolutism was not just a question of curial politics. Some of the most vociferous representatives of the idea of the council (such as Enea Silvio Piccolomini, later Pius II) supported the papacy for opportunistic reasons. In particular the cardinals, all nominated by the pope, often preferred the Curia to the council. But after the council, too, bishops and abbots did not think of allowing the 'lower clergy' and the laity to take part in the decision-making process of the church. And the secular monarchs were even more afraid of conciliar ('democratic') ideas and were therefore more interested in the preservation of the ecclesiastical status quo than in the reform of the papacy.

So, untroubled by the decrees of the council, the popes renewed their medieval claims. Even that former 'conciliarist' Piccolomini, now Pius II, was not ashamed officially to prohibit the appeal from the pope to a council and to punish it with excommunication. Of course such threatening gestures from the Curia were not taken very seriously in the church of the time, which was orientated towards the council. But Rome indefatigably continued to ignore and suppress the decrees of the Council of Constance. And on the very eve of the Reformation, at the Fifth Lateran Council in 1516, Leo X could bluntly declare: 'The Roman pontifex existing at the time, who has authority over all councils...'

At that time the ecumenicity of this papal council, made up almost exclusively of Italians and members of the Curia, was already disputed. And no pope has ever ventured to repeal the unpopular decree *Haec sancta* on the supremacy of the council or to declare that it is not universally binding because of the damage that would do to the notion of papal infallibility. That would be to saw off the support for the legitimacy of the Holy See on which the pope was sitting. What was the result of the controversy? It was doubly unsatisfactory. Extreme conciliarism without authentic primatial leadership of the church led to schism (at the Council of Basel, 1431–49), but extreme papalism without conciliar control led to a misuse of office (the Renaissance papacy).

Renaissance, but not for the church

Who would dispute that the Renaissance, beginning with Giotto and ending with Michelangelo, from the Florentine early Renaissance of the Quattrocento and the Roman high Renaissance of the Cinquecento up to the Sack of Rome in 1527, represents one of those rare climaxes of human culture? Names and works immediately come to mind: Bramante, Fra Angelico, Botticelli, Raphael and Leonardo da Vinci ... Since the French historian Jules Michelet and the Basle historian Jakob Burckhardt, 'Renaissance' has been understood not only as a movement in art history but as a term for an era in cultural history which saw the rise of humanist values.

It has proved difficult to make a precise demarcation between the Middle Ages and the Renaissance. Indeed, the Renaissance was more an important intellectual and cultural current within the late Middle Ages. The enthusiastic return to antiquity, to Graeco-Roman literature and philosophy (especially Plato), art and science played a decisive role. Classical education became the common property of the Italian elite and displaced medieval scholasticism. Antiquity provided the criterion for the detachment of men and women from many medieval norms of life and for a new self-confidence. But with a few exceptions, the Renaissance was not simply opposed to Christianity as 'new paganism'. The Renaissance developed within the social framework of Christianity. Not only Bernardino (Siena) and Savonarola (Florence), the great preachers of penitence, but also the greatest humanists – Nicholas of Cusa, Marsilio Ficino, Erasmus of Rotterdam and Thomas More – were concerned for a *renovatio Christianismi* and a lay piety in the spirit of reforming humanism and the Bible, which from the fourteenth century could increasingly be read in the vernacular.

The Renaissance popes, now again all Italians, once more with an Italianized Curia, were concerned above all with Italian affairs. All that was left of their former ambitions to rule the world was a moderate territorial state in Italy, which together with the Duchy of Milan, the republics of Florence and Venice and the kingdom of Naples, made up the five *principati*. In these circumstances, the popes wanted at last, through their large-scale building activity and encouragement of art, to indicate that the capital of Christianity was at least also the centre of art and culture.

But these extraordinarily expensive activities were purchased at the cost of a refusal to reform the church, which would have presupposed a fundamental change of disposition on the part of the totally secularized popes and the members of their Curia. These popes, who proved to be quite ordinary Italian Renaissance princes, were clearly to blame for the fact that the Renaissance resulted in no rebirth of the church. With unscrupulous *realpolitik* they ruled the church state as an Italian principality which belonged to them. They shamelessly preferred their own nephews or bastard children and attempted to establish dynasties in the form of hereditary clan princedoms for the papal families of Riario, della Rovere, Borgia and Medici.

The system was institutionalized hypocrisy. The Renaissance popes maintained celibacy for 'their' church with an iron hand, but no historian will ever discover how many children these 'holy fathers' fathered, living in monstrous luxury, unbridled sensuality and uninhibited vice. Three examples may suffice:

• The corrupt Franciscan della Rovere, Sixtus IV, sponsor of the dogma of the 'immaculate conception' of Mary, provided for whole hosts of nephews and favourites at the expense of the church and elevated six relatives to be cardinals, including his cousin Pietro Riario, one of the most scandalous wastrels of the

Roman Curia, who died of his vices at the early age of twenty-eight.

• Innocent VIII, who with his Bull gave a powerful stimulus to the witch craze, had his illegitimate children publicly recognized and celebrated their marriages with splendour and glory in the Vatican.

• The crafty Alexander VI Borgia, Machiavelli's model, who made his way into office with simony in the grand style and had four children by his mistress (and also other children by other women when he was still a cardinal), excommunicated Girolamo Savonarola, the great preacher of penitence, and was responsible for authorizing his burning in Florence.

It was said that under Alexander VI, Venus ruled; under his successor Julius II (1503–13) della Rovere, who was constantly waging war, Mars. Pope Leo X, who had been made cardinal at the age of thirteen by his reprobate uncle Innocent VIII, was above all fond of art; he enjoyed life and concentrated on acquiring the Duchy of Spoleto for his nephew Lorenzo. In 1517 he failed to see the significance of an event which was to usher in the end of the universal claim of the pope in the West as well. As Professor of New Testament in Wittenberg, an unknown Augustinian monk who had been in Rome a few months previously and who saw himself as a loyal Catholic published ninety-five critical theses against the trade in indulgences aimed at financing the gigantic new St Peter's which was now being built. His name was Martin Luther.

Reformation

For centuries Rome blocked any reform and now it got the Reformation, which quickly developed a tremendous religious, political and social dynamism. For Rome, which had already lost the East, this was a second catastrophe which cost it virtually all the northern half of its Roman empire. And with the loss of unity, of course, the catholicity of this church was also put in question. For however catholicity is to be understood (whether the approach is original and holistic, polemical and doctrinal, or geographical, numerical and cultural), one could not now overlook the fact that the all-embracing 'Catholic Church' was no longer the same as it was before the split and that with its unity, its catholicity, however that may be interpreted in theological terms, also seemed to be broken. Soon even Catholics would call their church the 'Roman Catholic' Church, without noting that the qualification 'Roman' fundamentally denied the 'Catholic': a true oxymoron.

The Reformers very clearly perceived the threat that they posed to catholicity. Martin Luther in particular vigorously resisted any move to make his name an attribute of the church. Nevertheless he was unsuccessful: some churches still call themselves 'Lutheran'. From the beginning, for both theological and legal reasons (the recognition of their church by imperial law), the Reformers attached importance to belonging to the 'Catholic Church'. Here, however, they understood this catholicity above all in a doctrinal sense: catholic faith was what was believed always, everywhere and by all, according to scripture.

Martin Luther was in no way from the start the un-Catholic rebel that for centuries Roman polemic and church historiography have made him. More recently Catholic historians, like Joseph Lortz, have brought the Catholic Luther to light. They have shown how Luther's understanding of the justification of the sinner was rooted in Catholic piety, concentrated on the crucified Christ whom Luther encountered in his Augustinian monastery; how the theology of Augustine in particular opened Luther's eyes to the corruption of sin as human self-seeking and the perversion of the self, but also to the omnipotence of the grace of God. Combined with this was medieval mysticism and its sense of being humble, small, nothing before God, to whom all honour was due. Even Luther's roots in the Ockhamism of the Tübingen scholar Gabriel Biel, whose pupil B. A. von Usingen was Luther's teacher, are now seen in a positive light: the understanding of grace as God's favour, the event of justification as an event of judgement, resting on the acceptance of men and women by a free divine election which has no foundation in them.

So Luther, who was rooted in the Catholic tradition in many ways, should by no means have been condemned sweepingly as un-Catholic. But the Vatican commission, which consisted almost entirely of canon lawyers, was neither able nor willing to see what was common to him and to the Catholic tradition. However, the critical discussion is not only about the 'Catholic Luther' – a Luther who is still Catholic or remained Catholic – but also about the Reformer Luther, who with Paul and Augustine attacked scholasticism and Aristotelianism. Here the criterion for judgement cannot simply be the Counter-Reformation Council of Trent, the theology of high scholasticism or Greek and Latin patristics; in the end, scripture, the gospel, the original Christian message, must be the primary, fundamental and permanently binding criterion of any Christian theology, including Catholic theology.

Was the programme of the Reformation Catholic?

Luther's personal impetus towards reform, and his tremendous historical explosive effect, derive from one source: he called on the church to return to the gospel of Jesus Christ, which he had experienced as a living gospel in Holy Scripture and especially in the writings of Paul. Specifically, this meant:

– As opposed to all the traditions, laws and authorities which have grown up over the centuries, Luther emphasized the primacy of scripture: 'scripture alone'.

– As opposed to all the thousands of saints and thousands upon thousands of official mediators between God and human beings, Luther emphasized the primacy of Christ: 'Christ alone', who is the centre of scripture and the point of orientation for all exegesis of scripture.

– As opposed to all pious religious achievements and efforts by men and women ('works') to attain the salvation of their souls, which were ordained by the church, Luther emphasized the primacy of grace and faith: 'grace alone', the grace of the gracious God – as it had been shown in the cross and resurrection of Jesus Christ – and 'faith alone', the unconditional trust of men and women in this God.

There is no question that by comparison with the 'thinking in storeys' characteristic of scholasticism, Luther's theology was far more confrontational: faith was opposed to reason, grace to nature, the Christian ethic to natural law, the church to the world, theology to philosophy, the distinctively Christian to the humanistic.

Initially in the monastery, over many years, Luther had come to know the private distress of conscience of a monk tormented by the awareness of being a sinner and of predestination. The message of justification on the basis of trusting faith had freed him from this. But he was concerned with more than a privatistic peace of the soul. His experience of justification formed the basis for his public appeal to the Catholic Church for reform. This was to be a reform in the spirit of the gospel, which was aimed less at the reformulation of a doctrine than at the renewal of Christian life in all spheres.

In 1520, for Martin Luther the year of his theological breakthrough, four theological works, appropriate to the situation, confidently chosen and with great theological power, showed the coherence and consistency of the Reformation programme. In addition to his edifying sermon 'On Good Works' (and trust in faith) and his writing 'On the Freedom of a Christian' (a summary of his understanding of justification), it was Luther's passionate appeal to the emperor, rulers and nobility for the reform of the church which caused the greatest stir. Entitled 'To the Christian Nobility of the German Nation on the Improvement of the Christian State', it again took up the *gravamina* (charges) of the German nation which had already been expressed so often.

This was the sharpest attack so far on the curial system, which was preventing a reform of the church with its three Roman presumptions ('The walls of the Romanists'): 1. That spiritual authority stood above worldly authority; 2. That the pope alone was the true interpreter of scripture; 3. That the pope alone could convene a council. According to Luther, none of this could be justified in any way from scripture and the old Catholic tradition. At the same time, Luther developed a reform programme in twenty-eight points which was as comprehensive as it was detailed. The first twelve demands applied to the reform of the papacy: renunciation of claims to rule the world and the church; independence of the emperor and the German church; and an end to the many forms of exploitation by the Curia. But then the programme became one for the reform of the life of the church and the world generally: monastic life, the celibacy of priests, indulgences, masses for souls, feasts of saints, pilgrimages, the mendicant orders, universities, schools, care of the poor, the abolition of luxury. Here already were the programmatic statements about the priesthood of all believers and church ministry, which was based on a commission to exercise publicly the priestly authority that was intrinsically given to all.

A further programmatic writing from the same year, 'On the Babylonian Captivity of the Church', was devoted to a new basis for the doctrine of the sacraments, the very foundation for Roman church law. Luther's argument was that if one took 'institution by Jesus Christ himself' as the sole criterion, there were only two sacraments in the strict sense – baptism, eucharist – and at best three – also penance. The other four – confirmation, ordination, marriage and final unction – could be retained as pious church customs, but not as sacraments instituted by Christ. Here again there were many practical proposals for reform – from communion with the chalice for the laity to the remarriage of innocent parties in a divorce. But need such demands have led to a break?

Responsibility for the split

Of course, everything depended on how, after centuries of obstruction, Rome reacted to the demands for a now understandably radical reform. Had people in the Vatican been able to recognize the signs of the time, they would have resolved to repent in the last hour, to reflect on the gospel of Jesus Christ, as it was bindingly laid down in Holy Scripture even for those who held office in the church. Of course they could have criticized Luther's excesses: his formulations were often emotionally one-sided and exaggerated. Rome could have called for both elaborations and corrections. But, at the same time, a fundamental reorientation would have been unavoidable for Rome. I know today that an agreement could have been arrived at over the matter of justification, as I argued in my doctoral dissertation *Justification* in 1957, and as has been confirmed by the consensus document produced in 1999 after the Roman Catholic–Lutheran conversations.

But what the quite serious Innocent III, confronted with Francis of Assisi, sought to avoid, did not even dawn on the superficial playboy Leo X. A Rome unwilling to reform responded to the Reformer's demand for a 'return to the gospel of Jesus Christ' as simplistically as ever with the demand for 'submission to the teaching of the church', presupposing that the church, the pope and the gospel were identical. What did a heretical young monk from the distant north count for in the face of the pope of Rome, the lord of the church, who still had the support of the worldly powers? It was quite clear that the monk had to recant: this was Rome's position – otherwise he would be burned at the stake like Hus, Savonarola, and hundreds of 'heretics' and 'witches'.

Anyone who has studied this whole story can have no doubt that it was not the Reformer Luther but Rome, unwilling for reform – and its German minions (notably the theologian Johannes Eck) – which was mainly to blame for the fact that the dispute about the right way to salvation and the practical reflection of the church on the gospel very rapidly turned into a different dispute, about the authority and infallibility of pope and councils. In view of the burning of the Reformer Jan Hus and the prohibition at the Council of Constance of the laity drinking from the chalice at the eucharist, this was an infallibility which Luther could not in any way affirm.

We must see the decisive point here: more than anyone before him in the fifteen hundred years of church history, Luther had found a direct existential access to the apostle Paul's doctrine of justification of the sinner by faith alone, and not through works. This had been completely distorted by the promotion of indulgences in the Catholic Church, which claimed that the sinner could be saved by performing set penances and even making payment of money. This rediscovery of Paul's message of justification – among the shifts, obscurities, cover-ups and over-paintings – is an astounding theological achievement, which the Reformer himself always recognized as the special grace of God. Simply in the light of this central point, a formal rehabilitation of Luther and the repeal of his excommunication by Rome is overdue. It is one of those acts of reparation which should follow the pope's confession of guilt today.

From the perspective of the present day we can understand the Reformation better as a paradigm change: a change in the overall constellation of theology, church and society. No less than the Copernican revolution in the change from a geocentric to a heliocentric picture of the world, Luther's Reformation was a major change from the medieval Roman Catholic paradigm to the Protestant-Evangelical paradigm: in theology and the church it was a move away from the all too human ecclesiocentricity of the powerful church to the christocentricity of the gospel. Above all, Luther's Reformation emphasized the freedom of Christians.

In such a significant process of transformation, methods, problem areas and attempts at a solution were restated; basic concepts ('justification', 'grace', 'faith') were redefined, and the material categories of scholastic philosophy deriving from

Aristotle (act and potency, form and matter, substance and accidents) were replaced by personal categories (gracious God, sinful man, trust, confidence). A new understanding of God, human beings, the church and the sacraments was made possible by a biblical and christocentric rethinking of theology.

The inner coherence, elementary transparency and pastoral effectiveness of Luther's answers, the new simplicity and creative eloquence of Lutheran theology, fascinated and convinced many. Because of the spread of the craft of printing, a flood of sermons and pamphlets and the German hymn spread and rapidly became popular. Moreover Luther's translation of the whole Bible into German, from the original texts, had a tremendous impact not only on the course of the Reformation but on the German language itself and over a much wider area. However, for many traditional Roman Catholics Luther's radical criticism of the medieval form of Christianity, the Latin sacrifice of the mass and private masses, the ministry of the church, the concept of the priest and monasticism, the law of celibacy and other traditions (the cult of relics, the veneration of the saints, pilgrimages, masses for souls) went too far and was said to be apostasy from true Christianity.

Basically, however, even then the learned Roman and German opponents of Luther could have seen where Luther was right, had they not put the words and the interests of the pope above the understanding of scripture. They could have recognized that Luther preserved the substance of faith, that despite all the radical changes there was a fundamental continuity of faith, rite and ethics; indeed, that there were still the same constants of Christianity as those of the medieval Roman Catholic paradigm: the same gospel of Jesus Christ, his God the Father and the Holy Spirit; the same initiation rite of baptism; the same communal celebration of the eucharist; the same ethic of the discipleship of Christ. To this degree there was only a paradigm change, and not a change of faith.

What was to be done next? Rome could still excommunicate the Reformer, but it could not stop the radical reshaping of church life in accordance with the gospel through the Reformation which was progressing and stirring up the whole of Europe. Nor could a potentially important 'third force' – alongside the first, Rome, and the second, Luther's Wittenberg – that conciliatory Catholic humanism and 'evangelism', which was associated above all with the name of Erasmus of Rotterdam, establish itself. This was not least because committed public resistance and steadfastness was not the style of Erasmus and the Erasmians: later the Erasmian Reginald Pole, cousin of Henry VIII of England and cardinal, would fail to be elected pope for lack of resolve. Instead, the next pope would be Cardinal Caraffa, the exponent of the conservative reactionary group and founder of the central Roman Inquisition, who would have even reforming cardinals like Morone imprisoned in Castel San Angelo.

In Germany the new paradigm of theology and church was soon solidly established. Luther attempted, to the best of his ability, to consolidate the Reformation movement inwardly: its worship by the 'Little Book of Baptism', the 'Little Wedding Book' and the 'German mass'; its religious education by the 'Greater Catechism' for pastors and the 'Lesser Catechism' for household use together with his translation of the Bible; its church constitution by a new church order promulgated by the ruler of the land. All in all, this was an amazing achievement by a single theologian. It could no longer be overlooked that after the great split in the all-embracing Catholic Church between East and West, a second had taken place in the West between North and South. The effects on state, society, economy, science and art were unmistakable. The Reformation pressed on.

At the end of Luther's life in 1547, the future of the church of the Reformation seemed far less rosy to him than it had in the year of his great breakthrough in 1520. The original enthusiasm of the Reformation had run out of steam. Community life was often in dire straits, not least because of the lack of pastors. Had people become so much better as a result of the Reformation? That was a question many were asking. Nor could the terrifying impoverishment of art – with the exception of music – be overlooked. Granted, the families of pastors became the social and cultural centre of the community, but the 'universal priesthood' of believers was hardly realized; rather, the gulf between clergy and laity was maintained in another form.

In addition, the Protestant camp could not preserve its unity. From the beginning there were numerous groups, communities, assemblies and movements which pursued their own strategies in implementing the Reformation. Even in Luther's lifetime there was a first split of Protestantism into a 'left-wing' and a 'right-wing' Reformation.

The 'left-wing' Reformation of the radical nonconformists ('enthusiasts') was made up of religious and social movements, mostly of anti-clerical laity, who also turned against the power of the state where they were persecuted. The Peasant Wars, condemned by Luther, must be seen in this context, as must Anabaptism, which the Swiss religious reformer Zwingli opposed in Zurich. In the end this tradition led to the development of the Free Churches, which assembled in their own places of worship: they had a voluntary membership of their own church order, financing themselves.

The 'right-wing' Reformation comprised the churches of the

authorities. The ideal of free Christian churches was not realized even in Luther's sphere of activity. As the Reformation churches had no bishops, the rulers transformed themselves into 'emergency bishops' and soon into *summepiscopi* who were in control of everything: the local ruler was something like a pope in his own territory. Thus, in Germany, the Reformation did not so much prepare the way for modernity, freedom of religion and the French Revolution as for state churches, the authority of the state and the absolutism of the ruler. This rule by princes and (in the cities) by magistrates only came to a well-deserved end in Germany with the revolution after the First World War.

Also during Luther's lifetime there was a second split, between Lutherans and 'Reformed': Huldrych Zwingli in Zurich, who parted company with Luther over eucharistic doctrine, stood for that consistent type of Reformation which John Calvin would then embody and realize in an exemplary way in Geneva: Reformed Christianity. Calvin was concerned to achieve not only a more or less thorough renovation but a systematic rebuilding of the church, a comprehensive reform of doctrine and life. In contrast to the Lutheran 'half-measures', the Reformation was to be carried through consistently, from the abolition of crucifixes, images and liturgical garments to the elimination of the mass, the organ, singing in church and altars, along with the processions and relics, confirmation and final unction; the eucharist was to be limited to four Sundays a year. So much for the Middle Ages!

John Calvin, originally a lawyer and not a theologian, presented an elementary, clear introduction to Reformation Christianity in his basic work *Institutio Religionis Christianae* as early as 1535; constantly corrected up to its final edition of 1559, it developed into the most significant Christian dogmatics between those of Thomas Aquinas and the German Friedrich

Schleiermacher. Certainly, with its doctrine of eternal pre-destination of a whole part of humankind to damnation, it came up against resistance everywhere. But in its revaluation of everyday work, practical involvement in the world and good works as a sign of election, it beyond doubt provided psy-chological conditions for what Max Weber called the typically 'modern capitalistic spirit'. And even if there could be no ques-tion of freedom of religion in Geneva – inquisition, torture and death by fire were instituted even there – it was indirectly of great significance for the development of modern democracy, especially in North America.

Thus in the course of the Reformation, three very different types of Protestant Christianity emerged: Lutheran, Reformed and Free Church. To these must be added a fourth, even more important, type, Anglicanism. Henry VIII's 'Reformation' of England was quite certainly not just a matter of a divorce, as the Catholic side often describes it, nor was it a popular movement, as in Protestant Germany. Above all it was a deci-sion of Parliament, carried through by the king. Instead of the pope, the king (and under him the Archbishop of Canterbury) was now the supreme head of the Church of England. That meant a break with Rome, but not with the Catholic faith.

Moreover the Anglican state church did not become Prot-estant in its life and constitution, after the German model. Only after Henry's death did the learned Archbishop of Canterbury Thomas Cranmer carry through what no bishop in Germany had succeeded in doing: a Reformation which maintained the episcopal constitution. To be specific:

– There was a simplified and concentrated liturgy in the spirit of the Bible and the early church (Book of Common Prayer, 1549).

– There was a traditional confession of faith with an evangelical doctrine of justification and a Calvinist doctrine of the eucharist (which is later toned down) (Forty-Two Articles, 1552).

– There was a reform of discipline, but without giving up the traditional structures of ministry.

After the years of the bloody Catholic reaction of Mary Tudor (Archbishop Cranmer, too, went to the stake), under Mary's half-sister Elizabeth I (1558–1603) a definitive form of that reformed Catholicism was achieved which, in a typically English way, combined the medieval and the Reformation paradigms of Christianity. Liturgy and church customs were reformed, but teaching and practice remained Catholic (as laid down in the Thirty-Nine Articles). Hence, to the present day, the Anglican Church regards itself as the middle way between the extremes of Rome and Geneva. The Act of Tolerance of William III of Orange after the 'Glorious Revolution' -- exactly one hundred years before the French Revolution – made possible independent denominations within and alongside the Anglican state church, Free Churches, which with their repudiation of the state church realized the autonomy of the congregation or individual community. In the United States of America the future was to belong to these 'Congregationalists' – together with the Baptists and later, above all, the Methodists.

The collapse of the Roman system which the Reformers expected in an apocalyptic, end-time mood, failed to materialize. Amazingly, a Catholic reform movement slowly developed. However, it did not originate in Germany or in Rome, but in Spain. In one and the same historic year, 1492, with the conquest of Muslim Granada, Spain, uniting Aragon and Castile, completed its Christian Reconquista, and with the discovery of America (Mexico was conquered in 1521) it ushered in its *Siglo de oro*, its proud 'golden century'. Granted, Spain was a land of the Inquisition: under the Grand Inquisitor Torquemada there were around nine thousand *autos-da fé* (acts of faith): burnings of heretics and Jews. But Spain was also a land of reform: under the humanistic cardinal primate Cisneros, even before the Reformation, as a result of the influence of Erasmus there was a renewal of the monásteries and the clergy, and the University of Alcala was founded.

And there was the Spanish King Charles I, famous throughout the world as the Emperor Charles V, the last great representative of a universal empire, on whose Habsburg empire – from the Balkans through Vienna and Brussels to Madrid, Mexico and Peru – the sun literally never set. Born in Ghent, Charles was brought up by the Erasmian Hadrian of Utrecht, later the last German-speaking pope, Hadrian VI. In his pontificate, which sadly lasted only eighteen months, Hadrian VI delivered into the hands of the Diet of Nuremberg in 1522 a far clearer confession of sins than John Paul II at the beginning of the twenty-first century: 'We are well aware that for some years now many abominable things have taken place at this Holy See: abuses in matters spiritual, transgressions of the commandments; indeed that all has turned for the worse. So it is not surprising that the sickness has spread from the head to the members, from the pope to the prelates. All of us, prelates and clergy, have departed from the right way.'

So Charles V, who when the Dominican Bartolomé de Las Casas objected, abandoned the further conquest of Latin America and allowed a public debate about its legal and moral basis, was not a medieval fanatic and hunter of heretics. But with all his convictions and power he stood up for the unity of the church and the traditional faith which had been handed down to him. He became the great opponent of the Reformers, but also of the popes, from whom he virtually had to wrest a council and reform.

Meanwhile, in Italy, too, initially inconspicuous circles who thought in terms of the gospel were able to gain influence. Certainly the plundering over many days by numerous marauding imperial troops in the Sack of Rome in 1527 brought the end of Roman Renaissance culture, but it did not bring any reform of the Roman Church. It was only Pope Paul III from the Farnese family (1533–49), still himself wholly a Renaissance man, with children and grandchildren as cardinals, who brought about the change in Rome. He appointed the leaders of the reform party, a series of capable and deeply religious men, to the college of cardinals: the layman Contarini and Pole, Morone and Caraffa, who worked out a proposal for reform. He confirmed the novel *Compañía de Jesús*, the Society of Jesus formed by the Basque officer Ignatius de Loyola. With an active spirituality, turned towards the world (the basis of which is laid down in the little book, *Spiritual Exercises*), the Jesuits, who had no distinctive dress for their order, no fixed place and no choral prayer, but were bound by strict discipline and unconditional obedience to God, the pope and their superiors in the order, became the carefully selected, thoroughly trained and thus effective elite order of the Counter-Reformation; the Capuchins, Oratorians and other orders were active in preaching to the people and in pastoral care.

Finally, in 1545 (almost three decades after the outbreak of the Reformation and only two years before Luther's death), with the assent of the emperor, Paul III opened the long-called-for new council, the Council of Trent.

After that there slowly developed, in characteristic opposition to the Protestant Christianity of Northern and Western Europe, a Mediterranean Catholicism with an Italian and Spanish stamp.

It not only gained influence in the Catholic country of Germany but was transferred to the lands of the Indios, soon called 'Latin America'. However, there it did not develop a truly indigenous form. The newly-discovered continents had no positive influence of any kind on Rome until the middle of the twentieth century, and cannot be the subject of separate treatment in the framework of this short history.

The Roman Catholic Counter-Reformation

After the Reformation, the papacy was on the defensive and condemned itself to reaction. As early as 1542, under Cardinal Carofa, the notorious Sanctum Officium Sanctissimae Inquisitionis, today called the Congregation for the Doctrine of Faith, was founded as the centre of the Inquisition of all countries, and a first Index of prohibited books was issued. This was a tragic development for Catholic Reformers of an evangelical disposition, and it was sealed by the election of the selfsame Carofa as pope in 1555. As Paul IV, he again attempted to set up a medieval theocracy, and failed lamentably.

From the beginning, the Italian friends of reform had little to say at the council, which finally met in Trent, in northern Italy, from 1545 to 1563. In contrast to the earlier, truly ecumenical councils, and in contrast to the Council of Constance, this was again a papal council, like the medieval general synods. At first, essentially only Italian and Spanish prelates took part; the Protestants understandably refused to participate.

However, the serious efforts at reform by this council cannot be overlooked; they would have their effect in the course of the following decades. Doctrinal decrees, wanted by Rome, on scripture and tradition, justification, the sacraments, purgatory and indulgences, removed some misunderstandings. Disciplinary decrees, required by the emperor, formed the basis for new forms of priestly education (on the model of the Pontificium Collegium Germanicum, similarly founded by Ignatius), the life of the religious orders and preaching. In time the reform decrees also led to the renewal of pastoral care, missions, catechesis and the care of the poor and the sick.

But the council said no word about the reform of the papacy, which was so urgently needed, though it did not say anything about papal primacy and infallibility either. The Roman Curia was all too afraid of the decrees of the Council of Constance about the supremacy of the council over the pope. Moreover, their renewal was called for at a later session of the council by leading German bishops and delegates from evangelical territories – though as vainly as the abolition of the oath of loyalty from bishops to the pope.

A militant demarcation from Protestantism now formed the external framework and the substantive limit of the renewal within Catholicism. The breakthrough of Catholic reform had in fact come about only under the pressure of the Reformation. The Reformation was thus not only the occasion for the gathering of the church at Trent, as some Catholic church historians think; it also challenged the Reformation, accelerated it and was its permanent opponent. The Counter-Reformation did not begin, as the Catholic conciliar historian Hubert Jedin thinks, only seventy-five years after the convening of the Council of Trent, but with the council itself. Catholic self-reform and militant Counter-Reformation were not two phases, but only two sides of the same reform movement. The council reacted to the theological concern of the Reformation with dozens of anathemas and demands for excommunication, and even the practical concerns of the Reformers, which were partly also shared by the emperor and numerous Catholic Reformers – the chalice for the laity, the liturgy in the vernacular and the marriage of priests – were rejected without serious discussion; only the Second Vatican Council four hundred years later would at least concern itself with the first two.

The basic anti-Reformation attitude of the Council of Trent was most clearly visible in its decrees on the sacraments, the Roman doctrine of the sacraments being the basis for Roman church law. With a total lack of concern for all exegetical, historical and theological objections from the Reformers, the sacraments were defined, under threat of excommunication, as seven, the medieval number: not only baptism, eucharist and penance but also confirmation, ordination, marriage and final unction were said to be sacraments personally 'instituted' by Christ. At the same time the medieval mass was restored, freed only from its most monstrous excrescences, and now was controlled to the last word and position of the priest's finger by 'rubrics' (stage directions printed in red). This totally regulated liturgy of the clergy, then often celebrated in baroque fashion at the time, would remain the basic form of the Catholic liturgy down to the Second Vatican Council – alongside the ever more numerous devotions, the quite lively popular piety of processions and pilgrimages, and the heightened veneration of Mary.

Thus for the Council of Trent (in contrast to Vatican II), reform within the church was a function of the programme of the fight against the Reformation and not of reconciliation and reunion. That was also expressed in art: the grandiose architecture, sculpture, painting and music of the baroque were an expression of the reinforced claim to rule of an *Ecclesia militans et triumphans* and, at the same time, the last unitary style of ancient Europe. Generally speaking, the Catholic reform bore the stamp of restoration. It was the medieval spirit in Counter-Reformation garb. This was also true of what Jedin calls the 'resurgence of scholasticism' in Spain and in Rome and the now novel 'controversial theology' against the Protestants.

So the Council of Trent could not and would not be the ecumenical council of union for the whole of Christianity (or at least Western Christianity) which had been desired and called for for so long. It was rather the particular confessional council of the Counter-Reformation and was now utterly at the service of the re-Catholicizing of Europe. This would be carried through politically wherever possible and with military force wherever necessary. Diplomatic pressure combined with military intervention: in the second half of the sixteenth century in Europe this strategy led to a real flood of acts of violence, 'battles of faith' and wars of religion (what a misuse of faith and religion!). In Italy and Spain the little Protestant groups were oppressed; in France there were eight civil wars against the Huguenots (three thousand Protestants were massacred in the St Bartholomew's Night massacre in Paris); in the Netherlands the Calvinist Dutch engaged in a fight for freedom against the Spanish rule of terror and there was a war between Spain and the Netherlands lasting for more than eighty years. Finally, Germany was riven by the fearful Thirty Years War (1618–48), which made it a battlefield of ruins not only for Catholics and Protestants, but also for Danes, Swedes and French.

The Peace of Westphalia in 1648 regulated the situation in Germany in accordance with the principle of the parity of the two confessions and the recognition of the Reformed Church. In essentials, the regions of the two confessions marked out then have remained until the present day. So too has the independence of Switzerland and the Netherlands from the German empire, which was recognized at that time in international law.

An era had now come to an end. The religious forces which had been called on to the maximum were largely exhausted. Religion had not led the way out of the hell of war. Rather, the religious dispute over the sole truth was a chief factor in the Thirty Years War. Peace could be concluded only by leaving faith aside. Christianity had shown itself incapable of peace. In so doing, it had decisively lost credibility, so that it now less and less formed the decisive religious, cultural, political and social bond of Europe. In this way it had itself contributed to the process of detachment from religion, of secularization, of increasing worldliness which would decisively determine the character of the new time, modernity. A new secular culture was in the making.

VII *The Catholic Church versus Modernity*

A new time

How different the Escorial, outside Madrid, is from the palace of Versailles! The Escorial is a solitary, cool, grey monastic palace in the bare hill-country of Castile, a royal residence, the seat of authority, a centre of scholarship and prayer, with the church at the centre; Versailles is a splendid château surrounded by a gigantic artificial garden landscape, a highly representative classical building with the 'Chambre du Roi' at the centre and the church in the wings. Their builders and lords were also truly different from each other: the Habsburg Philip II, a strictly orthodox Catholic through and through, the most powerful man of the second half of the sixteenth century, and the Bourbon Louis XIV, 'Catholic' but hardly really religious; rather, he was an utterly secularized autocrat, the most powerful figure of the second half of the seventeenth century.

Here were two rulers, two worlds, separated by the great watershed of recent European history around the middle of the seventeenth century.

• Spain was the pre-eminent Roman Catholic power, made rich by discoveries but exhausted by all too many wars: a defeat by France (1643) and the Peace of the Pyrenees (1659), the loss of the Netherlands (1648) and Portugal (1668). At the end of the century Spain had left the concert of European powers as a great power.

• Germany (after the Thirty Years War) and Italy (as a result of the fight between the discordant city states an easy prey for the great powers) were irrelevant to world politics.

• The papacy, which had been excluded as a regulatory authority in international law by the Peace of Westphalia, was not replaced by any new institution which transcended the state. But the power of Protestantism to engage in any offensives also seemed to be broken. The confession was subordinate to the state: the age of the confessions was replaced by the age of royal absolutism for almost one hundred and fifty years, from 1648 to 1789.

A new historical shift of balance took place: no longer, as in the time of the Reformation and Counter-Reformation, from the Mediterranean to Central Europe, but from the centre of Europe to the western periphery of the Atlantic nations: the Netherlands, France and England, which seized the 'free ocean' from Spain and Portugal for their fleets.

However, France was now the dominant European power. Under Louis XIII, son of the former Huguenot Henry IV, who was converted to Catholicism (declaring that 'Paris is worth a mass'), France remained a Catholic monarchy, but it became a largely secularized centralist power state, the most modern in Europe. This was the work of the omnipotent *premier ministre*, Cardinal Richelieu. Internally he established royal absolutism in the face of the nobility, Parliament and the peasants, and disempowered the Huguenots in political and finally military terms. But externally, in the face of Spanish armies, English fleets and German mercenary armies Richelieu established the dominance of France on the European continent by putting reasons of state above all interests of church and confession. For the first time he consistently implemented Machiavelli's principles of a *Realpolitik*. Wars for hegemony were built into this scheme, as were the vast costs of war, with all its consequences.

Under Louis XIV these principles of modern power politics – sovereign nation-state, reasons of state and the struggle for hegemony – were brought to a peak. Religion served to legitimate royal absolutism: instead of 'one God – one Christ – one faith', as in the Middle Ages, there was now *un Dieu – une foi – une loi – un roi*. Rationalistic political thinkers, both on the continent and in England, argued that royal absolutism was the only means of warding off chaos and guaranteeing internal peace through a strong central state (Thomas Hobbes, *Leviathan*, 1651). The state – in principle without any divine grace – was the natural product of a treaty between people and government – and treaties, as would be proved, were made to be broken.

At the same time France rose to become Europe's leading cultural influence: after the age of Spain came the age of France. French replaced Latin as a world language (and the language of treaties), and French classicism replaced the exuberant baroque. Everything was dominated by geometry, which became virtually a characteristic of the era: the state as a rationally constructed machine, from the building of cities and fortifications and the architecture of gardens to exercises, music and dance. All this was connected with the first of those revolutionary impulses which herald a turn of the ages, the epoch-making shift to modernity. Europe would no longer orientate itself, as in the Renaissance, using antiquity as its model, but rather using autonomous reason, technical progress and 'the nation'.

It is not surprising, then, that the paradigmatic innovations and 'modernization effects' in society, church and theology were mostly not to be found in the undisputed Roman sphere of rule. The Roman Catholic paradigm, which initially was so innovative in the Middle Ages, was increasingly being forced into a medieval straitjacket, even if the Roman system continued to function as an effective instrument of rule in Catholic countries. Since the Council of Trent, the church had increasingly shut itself up in the Roman Catholic 'bulwark' from which, in subsequent centuries, it attacked with ancient weapons like condemnations, bans on books, excommunications and suspensions the ever more numerous 'enemies of the church' who were storming it. It had little success: after a few important popes of the Counter-Reformation – from Pius V through Gregory XIII to Urban VIII in the second half of the sixteenth and the first half of the seventeenth century – in the second half of that century the papacy found itself increasingly in the shadow of history.

Protestantism may have threatened to rigidify to traditionalism, but despite everything people were better prepared for the new time than in triumphalistic Catholicism, which from the middle of the nineteenth century to the middle of the twentieth century was mostly to be overtaken by the intellectual movements of the day (with the exception of a few waves like Romanticism). There were several reasons for this:

• Despite all its baroque ornamentation, the Catholicism of the Counter-Reformation clearly represented a conservative religion of restoration; but in Protestantism, from its origins, there was a forward-looking tendency towards reform.

• On the whole, Catholicism remained the religion of the Romance people, who lagged behind in economics, politics and culture (with the exception of France) but Protestantism was the religion of the now rising German and Anglo-Saxon nations.

• In Catholicism the pope himself decided on the interpretation of the Bible and tolerated no deviation; in Protestantism, however, one could constantly refer to a Bible read independently and appeal to the decision of one's own conscience, in the face of the doctrinal statements of the church, and so develop an ethic of responsibility. The Reformation's 'freedom of a Christian' made a decisive contribution to the modern emphasis on responsibility, coming of age and autonomy.

The scientific and philosophical revolution: 'reason'

The revolution of modernity was primarily an intellectual revolution. As the English politician and philosopher Francis Bacon proclaimed at a very early stage, knowledge is power. And in fact science proved to be the first great power of rising modernity. What Bacon proclaimed, but still hardly provided any empirical or experimental basis for, was initiated methodologically by Galileo, Descartes and Pascal, who were followed by Spinoza, Leibniz and Locke, Newton, Huygens and Boyle. They all laid the foundations for the new sense of the superiority of reason, which promised a quasi-mathematical certainty.

The new, truly revolutionary world system which the Catholic cathedral dean Nicolaus Copernicus presented, purely theoretically and only as a hypothesis, seemed at first to pose a threat to the biblical word-view when the Italian Galileo Galilei irrefutably confirmed it with experiments. Thus Galileo became one of the founders of modern science, which demonstrated the laws of nature and heralded the boundless investigation of nature. Two generations later Isaac Newton constructed a convincing new world system quite rationally from many fragmentary elements and became the father of classical theoretical physics.

At the same time as Galileo, the mathematician and scientist

René Descartes laid the foundation for modern philosophy. The certainty of mathematics was now the new ideal of knowledge. The foundation of all certainty – specifically in radical doubt – is the fact of one's own existence, which can be experienced in the act of thinking: *Cogito, ergo sum*. This was a major turning-point: the place of original certainty had been shifted from God to human beings. Thus the argument no longer moved, as in the Middle Ages or the Reformation, from certainty about God to certainty about oneself, but in a modern way from certainty about oneself to certainty about God – if that is possible!

It was Immanuel Kant who, in a great philosophical synthesis, was able to combine continental rationalism and English empiricism and to construct the whole of reality consistently in the light of the human subject. In questions relating to the knowledge of God, Kant no longer appealed to 'theoretical' but to 'practical' reason, which manifests itself in human action: the question of God is not about a purely scientific knowing but about the moral action of human beings, for which the existence of God is the condition of its possibility.

What a change! In the medieval Roman Catholic paradigm the supreme authority was the pope, and in the Reformation the 'Word of God'; but in the modern paradigm it is *ratio, raison*. Human reason is modernity's leading value number 1. Reason now increasingly becomes the arbiter of all questions of truth. Only the rational is regarded as true, useful and binding. Philosophy is given precedence over theology; nature (natural science, natural philosophy, natural religion, natural law) over grace; the human over the specifically Christian.

The church and the Copernican shift

How did the church react to this 'Copernican shift' in science and philosophy? Luther and his fellow reformer, Melanchthon, rejected the work of Copernicus because it contradicted the Bible. But it was not until 1616 – when the Galileo case came to a head – that in Rome Copernicus was put on the Index of banned books. The Catholic Church now became an institution characterized not so much by intellectual effort, empirical assimilation and cultural competence as by defensiveness against all that was new. Censorship, the Index, the Inquisition were quickly brought on the scene. There were many notorious cases:

– Giordano Bruno, who combined the Copernican model of the world with a pantheizing Neoplatonic-mystical Renaissance piety, was burned in Rome in 1600;

– Similarly the Italian natural philosopher Lucilio Vanini, who was said to have taught the identity of God and nature, was burned in Toulouse in 1619;

– The anti-Aristotelian philosopher Tommaso Campanella wrote his utopian *City of the Sun* (1602) in the prison of the Inquisition; he was able to escape only two years later;

– Galileo Galilei, entangled in a trial by the Inquisition, finally recanted his 'errors' in 1633 as a loyal Catholic and lived the last eight years of his life under house arrest, still working on although he was blind.

Galileo's conflict with the church was a symptomatic precedent which poisoned at the roots its relationship with the new and rising natural sciences. His condemnation, carried through in the Catholic countries with all the means of denunciations and inquisitors, spread an atmosphere of fear, so that Descartes postponed indefinitely the publication of his treatise

On the World or *Treatise on Man*: it would not be published until fourteen years after his death. There was an almost silent emigration of natural science from the church. In the Catholic countries, hardly any later generations of scientists appeared.

The cultural and theological revolution: 'progress'

The scientific and philosophical revolutions had far-reaching effects on European society, where for so many centuries the church authorities had dominated all thought. They led to the cultural revolution of the Enlightenment, which finally also resulted in a political revolution. For the first time in the history of Christianity the impulses for a new paradigm of the world, society, church and theology did not come primarily from within theology and the church but from outside it. Now the human being as an individual was put at the centre, and at the same time the human horizon extended and differentiated itself almost infinitely: geographically by the discoveries of new continents, and physically through the telescope and the microscope.

Now the (old) word 'modern' became modern: the designation for a new sense of time. In the cultural change of climate there was a marked cooling-off over religion. Granted, in the seventeenth century, order, authority and discipline, church, hierarchy and dogma were still thought highly of. But behind the glittering façades of the state and the church they were abused unscrupulously by absolutist rulers and their devoted church leaders to develop their own power and splendour. A process of secularization and emancipation set in which would also extend to Germany, though in a watered-down form. In a momentous way, culture and religion, society and the church drifted apart.

The witty and sceptical polemicist and essayist Voltaire rejected all positive religion, hated the church (*écrasez l'infame*) and effectively interceded for tolerance even towards the Protestants (Huguenots). However, he was not an atheist. He also promoted the thirty-five-volume *Encyclopédie* – the monumental work of the French Enlightenment – which, as the *Summa* of modern knowledge, sought to bring together the Enlightenment criticism of state and church and set out to present human beings, nature and society in a rational way. This was the new mechanistic view of the world from a deistic perspective. There was still a belief in a Creator and Director of man the machine (though a very remote one). There could still have been an understanding between state and church if, from the church side, progress had been made towards a critical interpretation of the Bible in the light of the results of the new natural sciences and a more critical attitude towards the *ancien régime*.

Belief in the omnipotence of reason and the possibility of dominating nature developed: it became the foundation for the modern idea of progress. In the eighteenth century the secular idea of progress was extended to all spheres of life. The whole process of history appeared to be rationally progressive and progressively rational. Only now were new words coined like 'progress'. This was a mechanistic belief in progress, which could be understood in terms of both evolution and then also of revolution. Progress was assigned almost divine attributes like eternity, omniscience, omnipotence and all-goodness. Instead of an unchanging, static, hierarchical, eternal world order there was now the new unitary view of the world and history as representing permanent progress. Belief in progress now became modern leading value number 2, the realization of happiness already in this world. Human self-determination and human power over the world – a substitute religion for more and more people had been born.

The consequences of the Enlightenment for the church

Wars of religion were now increasingly thought to be as inhuman and unchristian as the burnings of witches. Medieval and Reformation belief in the devil, demons and magic no longer fitted the progressive age of reason. The witch trials and burnings were first attacked by the Jesuit Friedrich von Spee and then by the Protestant lawyer Christian Thomasius.

And like indulgences, pilgrimages, processions and monasteries, so too compulsory celibacy and Latin as the liturgical language came under fire. The Jesuit order, which had moved far from the ideal of its founder and entangled itself in the politics and business of this world, was widely hated as the agency of the papacy and the exponent of anti-modernity and finally, under pressure from the absolutist regimes of Portugal, Spain and France, was abolished by the pope himself. But the popes themselves – apart from Benedict XIV around the middle of the eighteenth century, who was friendly, social, learned and enlightened – had sunk into insignificance and reacted to the challenge of the time only with stereotyped responses, sterile protests and sweeping condemnations. The Catholic rulers, out of self-interest in the status quo, were often the only supporters of the papacy.

Christian theology, especially scholasticism, was not spared the cultural revolution in the name of the Enlightenment. Here biblical criticism took on a key role; now it examined even Holy Scripture with the tools of historical criticism. This approach was associated with the French Oratorian Richard Simon, a contemporary of Descartes and Galileo, who had learned from the Jewish biblical critic Baruch de Spinoza. Simon discovered that the 'five books of Moses' were in fact composed of different sources. They could not come from Moses, but were the product of a long historical development. Simon's critical history of the Old Testament of 1678 was immediately confiscated on the initiative of the famous court bishop and preacher Jacques-Bénigne Bossuet.

Thus the spirit of critical biblical research within the Catholic Church was crushed even before it could blossom. The result was the emigration from the Church of Rome of critical exegetes and thus of the intellectual avant-garde of theology in general. It was only through the tremendous work of generations initially limited to Protestant exegetes that the Bible came to be the best investigated book in the history of the world.

The religious tolerance which was also still remote from the concerns of the Reformers now also became a key watchword of modernity. Ever more accurate reports by explorers, missionaries and merchants from the new continents furthered the insight that the Christian religion was perhaps not such a unique phenomenon as was previously believed. Indeed, the more that international communication intensified through the discoveries of new countries, cultures and religions, the more in fact the relativity of Christianity, with its own European stamp, was demonstrated. The initially successful Catholic mission to China in the sixteenth and seventeenth centuries, initiated by the Italian Jesuit Matteo Ricci, who in clothing, language and behaviour assimilated completely to the Chinese Confucian way of living, was stopped as a result of a 'rites dispute' stirred up by rival Franciscans, Dominicans and the Inquisition: in a historic papal mistake, it was decreed that anyone who in the future wanted to remain, or to become, a Christian must cease to be a Chinese.

In Europe it was not a church document but Gotthold Ephraim Lessing's great Enlightenment play *Nathan the Wise* (1779) which programmatically showed the vision of peace among the religions as a presupposition of peace in humankind generally. Thus the notion of tolerance became established in the face of all confessionalism: instead of the monopoly of an individual religion and the rule of two confessions, now there was to be tolerance between the different Christian confessions and also between different religions. Freedom of conscience and the practice of religion stood right at the top of the list of human rights which were called for increasingly loudly, and which required political implementation.

The political revolution: 'nation'

The cultural revolution of the Enlightenment was followed by a revolution in politics, state and society. And the French Revolution was *the* revolution. Initially it was in no way directed against the Catholic Church: if the senior clergy, the First Estate, formed an alliance with the Second Estate, the nobility who were similarly unwilling for reform, the lower clergy formed an alliance with the Third Estate, the 98 per cent with no privileges. Their representatives constituted themselves as the *Assemblée nationale* in Versailles in 1789; this assembly boldly claimed to be the sole representative of the nation. When the crown reacted with a demonstration of power, there was a direct realization of the sovereignty of the people, without the king and finally against the king. This had long since been prepared for in theory by Rousseau and others.

Gone was the medieval theocracy embodied in the pope; gone, too, was the Protestant authority of a ruler or city council; gone, finally, was the early modern enlightened absolutism of a Frederick II or Joseph II. The hour of democracy now struck. The people (*demos*) itself, embodied in the national assembly, was sovereign. And the nation became modernity's leading value number 3.

However, the revolution was first carried through fully by the violent action of directed masses under the slogan of a programmatic ideology: *liberté* (political), *égalité* (social), *fraternité* (intellectual). It was only the revolt of the people and the storming of the Bastille on 14 July 1789 which compelled Louis XVI to recognize the revolution as legitimate and the National Assembly as sovereign. The storming of the châteaux by the rural masses spread great fear, and the annulling of all feudal rights by the National Assembly sealed the collapse of the *ancien régime*.

This cleared the way for the proclamation of the Declaration of Human and Civil Rights of 26 August 1789 – on the American model (1776). It is the Magna Carta of modern democracy, one of the great documents of human history. Catholic clergy also played a decisive part in the proclamation of human and civil rights. In the revolutionary Parliament, along with the Declaration of Rights (*droits*) not only the clergy but almost half the delegates called for the passing of a declaration of human responsibilities (*devoirs*) – something still to be desired today.

The church and the Revolution

Only after the King had been forced to move from Versailles to Paris on 5/6 October 1789 did the National Assembly, which had moved with him, now pass revolutionary resolutions against the church, the greatest, most powerful and richest body in the old system – first, above all, in order to clean up the rotten condition of state finances. This provoked counter-revolutionary movements, especially in the country, and these in turn further stirred up the mood of hostility towards the churches and religion among the Paris revolutionaries. Only now was church property nationalized; clergy incomes were limited, and all monasteries and religious orders were dissolved. Finally came a 'Civil Constitution of the Clergy', which adapted the boundaries of dioceses to the boundaries of departments, ordained the election of the pastor by all the citizens of the commune, and prescribed the nomination of the bishop by the administration of the department of state, along with an advisory body to the bishop made up of priests and laity.

The aim was a national church largely independent of Rome, in the spirit of the old Gallican freedoms. But this generated massive resistance among the clergy, which resulted in yet stronger radicalization on the other side. Every clergyman now also had to take an oath on the civil constitution; most bishops and around half the lower clergy refused to comply. All lost their offices. Of the victims of the September massacre of 1792, numbering between eleven and fourteen hundred, around three hundred were priests.

And what about Rome? Pius VI, himself an aristocrat, declared the 1791 civil constitution invalid and with a reference to divine revelation rejected the 'abominable philosophy of human rights' and especially freedom of religion, conscience and the press and the equality of all human beings. This was a fatal decision for the Catholic Church, though time and again it would be confirmed by Rome. Diplomatic relations between France and the Holy See were broken off; in 1798 the Roman Republic was proclaimed after French troops marched into Rome; Pope Pius VI was declared deposed and brought to France against his will. The Roman Catholic Church now appeared as the great foe of the revolutionary transformation, which for its part, with modern means like the guillotine (under Robespierre around sixteen thousand were executed in ten months) and the people's war to defend the Revolution, aimed at a total break with the past. Here was the utopia of a complete refounding of the social order and all institutions of the nation on reason alone.

The chief victim of the national revolution was the Catholic Church. It lost its secular power, which extended to education, hospitals and care for the poor, and also its tremendous property and a considerable proportion of its clergy (through emigration, execution and deportation). Instead of a culture governed by the church and clergy, a secularized, republican culture took root.

Granted, it proved impossible to establish the national civil constitution introduced by the Revolution, which called for a new reckoning of time (1792 = Year 1) and ten weekdays, and the replacement of Christian worship with the cult of 'Reason' (as a goddess) and then of the 'Supreme Being' in the cathedral of Notre Dame. These innovations disappeared only a few years after Robespierre was guillotined (1794). But some fundamental social changes endured, and these have shaped the mentality of people, at least in France, to the present day.

– The table of human rights replaced the Christian creed, and the state constitution replaced church law.

– The tricolour replaced the cross, and the civil register replaced church baptism, marriage and burial. Teachers replaced priests.

– The altar of the Fatherland, on which the patriot was to surrender his life, replaced the altar and the sacrifice of the mass. Patriotic names replaced many names of localities, towns and streets which had a religious colouring.

– The veneration of the heroized martyrs replaced the veneration of saints. The 'Marseillaise' replaced the Te Deum.

– The enlightened ethic of bourgeois virtues and social harmony replaced Christian ethics.

The osmosis which time and again was possible between Christianity and a new culture in the earlier paradigm changes was not at all wanted by Rome and the hierarchy, which was focused on the past; it was also systematically prevented by the revolutionaries, with their republican counter-culture. The result in France was the split between clericals and anti-clericals, indeed the formation of two hostile cultures: the new militant republican lay culture of the dominant liberal bourgeoisie and the deep-rooted Catholic-conservative, clerical and royalist, later papalist counter- or sub-culture of the church. The march of the official Catholic Church into a cultural ghetto had begun.

Was there an alternative? Above all, Abbé Henri-Baptiste Grégoire worked for a reconciliation of church and democracy in the spirit of the ideals of earliest Christianity; as a bishop he was a spiritual leader of the constitutional church. But this alternative did not have a chance. Many of Grégoire's concerns would be established only by the Second Vatican Council. Since then, it may also be stated openly that 'freedom, equality and brotherhood' – long vilified – have a foundation in primitive Christianity although, as we saw, this was overlaid in the church with hierarchical power structures at a very early stage. So should the church largely work as a bulwark of anti-democratic reaction and not in the spirit of its founder as a fellowship of free people, in principle equal, a fellowship of brothers and sisters?

However, the modern principle of the nation bestowed on Europe a highly pernicious ideology: that of nationalism and later of imperialism. Already for Napoleon Bonaparte, who ended and at the same time overcame the Revolution, who deposed Pius VI and made a concordat with Pius VII, eventually to deport him too to France, national expansion was more important than the Revolution's task of humanity. His wars of conquest cost hundreds of thousands of lives. The national principle suppressed the humane principle. And even if France, throughout the nineteenth century, dominated political developments with the great slogans of the Revolution, it did not remain the determining political power. Rather, it was Great Britain which became the leading world power in the nineteenth century. However, this was connected with another revolution which ushered in a modern economic system, indeed a new world civilization.

The technological and industrial revolution: 'industry'

England, which had carried through its Glorious Revolution and established Parliament as its political system a century before the French Revolution, initiated those technical and industrial revolutions which were to change the European world, and thus also Christianity, no less deeply than the political revolution.

After the terrors of the French Revolution and the devastating Napoleonic wars, a longing for the 'good old days' broke through everywhere. And there were numerous attempts to restore the old paradigm as 'the will of God' in both the Protestant and the Catholic spheres. Thus now, again, there was a defence of the monarchy as a form of state, of a society ordered by classes, of a hierarchical Roman Church, and of family and property as abiding basic values which in principle remained constant. On the basis of its resistance to Napoleon, the papacy, which guaranteed this, again became a moral authority.

At the Congress of Vienna in 1814–15, which was dominated by the 'Holy Alliance' of the conservative states of Austria (led by Chancellor Metternich), Russia and Prussia, the Roman Curia also took it for granted that it would get back the papal state abolished by Napoleon. The traditional *monsignori* economy was immediately reintroduced: the secular system of law (the Napoleonic Code) was abolished and the pre-modern papal legislation was restored. Seven hundred cases of 'heresy' were investigated by the Congregation for the Doctrine of Faith (the Holy Office). Thus in the nineteenth century the papal state was the most backward state in Europe both politically and socially; in it the pope even spoke out against railways, gas lighting, suspension bridges and the like.

Conservative social theorists like Edmund Burke in England, and writers like François de Chateaubriand and above all Joseph de Maistre, who in a much-read book *On the Pope* (1819) transferred the concept of sovereignty to the pope, supported such positions. At any rate it was the time of Romanticism which, initially progressive, now glorified the medieval social structure all over Europe and suppressed the Enlightenment, which seemed discredited by the excesses of the Revolution. But after the revolutionary wave of 1848, in which reaction once again proved victorious, both Restoration and Romanticism turned out to be a counter-revolutionary interlude.

Democracy continued its triumphal progress, and so did the technical revolution: lightning conductors, spinning machines, mechanical looms, steam engines fuelled with coal and at the same time the building of roads, bridges and canals, the development of the locomotive, the steamship, telegraphy and after 1825 the first railway line in England. All these were precursors for new methods of production and the organization of work. A highly significant change in the conditions of economic and social life began to come about. This was called the Industrial Revolution: a revolution in the sphere of technology, the processes of production, the production of energy, transport, the rural economy, the markets, but also in the sphere of social structures and thought. This was bound up with the population explosion, the agricultural revolution and headlong urbanization. In the first third of the nineteenth century, industrialization from England also embraced the Netherlands, Belgium, France and Switzerland; only in the middle of the century did it reach Germany and, finally, the rest of Europe, Russia and Japan. Industrial techniques, instead of being simply empirical as hitherto, were now implemented on a scientific basis, and became technology.

Made possible by science and technology, in the course of the nineteenth century industry developed along with democracy. It became modernity's leading value number 4. People now used the term 'industrial' and spoke of a bourgeois-capitalist 'industrial society', which replaced the lethargic aristocratic society and which was characterized by the virtue of 'industry'.

But new class conflicts developed out of the industrial capitalist process of production. Large parts of the working population were in great distress; they suffered under low wages, long working hours, miserable living conditions and social uncertainty, as well as from the exploitation of women and children at work. What was called the 'social question' became increasingly urgent; this was no coincidence, given the *laissez-faire* of the capitalistic 'Manchester liberalism'.

The proletariat reacted. In the second half of the nineteenth century, in the face of the unbounded domination of private capital, socialism developed. This was a heterogeneous socialist workers' movement, which extended from the French 'utopian' early socialists and the anarchists to the 'scientific socialism' of Karl Marx and Friedrich Engels. The Communist Manifesto was proclaimed in 1848. Instead of being concerned with freedom for the individual (the basic liberal concern), it was now increasingly concerned with social justice (the basic concern of socialism) and thus with another, juster social order. But what was the attitude of the Catholic Church to the Industrial Revolution and to social justice?

A sweeping condemnation of modernity – the Council of the Counter-Enlightenment

For the Catholic, Protestant and Anglican churches, the break with tradition brought about by democratization and industrialization came as a shock, but also as a challenge to win back, by a whole series of new forms of church action, the workers they had lost. In the nineteenth century there was beyond doubt a revival of religious forces in the clergy and laity, among the religious orders, in the missionary movement, in charitable work and education, and especially also in popular piety. The church associations, with a wealth of religious, social and indirectly political initiatives, were typical of this period, especially in Germany; chief among them was the Catholic People's Association, in fact the greatest Catholic association in the world.

In this way a significant social movement developed in German Catholicism, in particular under the influence of Bishop Wilhelm Emmanuel von Ketteler of Mainz. This made the church the advocate of the poor and the lower classes in need.

But even these social activities within the church finally lost credibility as a result of the controversies over the definition of papal infallibility at the First Vatican Council in 1870. The appropriateness of these was challenged as vigorously and unsuccessfully by Bishop Ketteler as by the majority in the German and French episcopates. In this discussion it became clear that modern democracy, which had largely abolished the absolutist system, and the Roman system, which was formed in the eleventh century and put a religious brake on absolutism, were in conflict, indeed were like fire and water. In democracies, the class system had disappeared; in the Roman system, the clergy had the upper hand by virtue of their status. In democracies, efforts were made to secure and establish human rights and civil rights; in the Roman system, human rights and the rights of Christians in the church were denied. In a representative democracy, the people was sovereign; in the Roman system, the people and clergy were excluded from the election of pastors, bishops and the pope. In a democracy, there was a division of authority (legislative, executive and judicial); in the Roman system, all authority was in the hands of the bishops and the pope (primacy and infallibility). In a democracy, there was equality before the law; the Roman system was a two-class system of clergy and laity. In a democracy, there was a free election of those with responsibilities at all levels; in the Roman system, there was nomination by the superior authority (bishops, the pope). In a democracy, Jews and those of other faiths were on an equal footing; in the Roman system, Catholicism was the religion of the state wherever it could be established.

The revolutionary wave which started from Paris in 1848 also engulfed the church state. To begin with, Pope Pius IX, elected two years earlier, fell in with liberal reforms, decreed an amnesty and was enthusiastically celebrated by the people. But because he shrank from consistent reforms, he was forced by rebels to fleet to Gaeta. After the defeat of the Italian revolution, with the help of French and Austrian troops he returned to Rome a different man. He had become the unyielding opponent of all 'liberal' movements (i.e., those which were well disposed towards reform), intellectual and cultural, in politics, thought and theology. Under him a paternalistic 'Ultramontanism', that emotional and sentimental veneration of the Holy Father 'over the mountains' which was unknown both in the Middle Ages and in the Counter-Reformation, spread through Northern and Western Europe. More and more congregations of men and women, associations (the 'Pius Association') and organizations of all kinds which were 'loyal to Rome', were active in the spirit of the Roman restoration and unconditional obedience to the pope. They reinforced the political polarization in society instead of overcoming it.

This was a short-sighted strategy: consolidation inside and isolation outside. Under the direction of Pius IX, an emotionally unstable man untroubled by intellectual doubt who evinced the symptoms of a psychopath, the medieval Counter-Reformation Catholic fortress was now built up against modernity with all available powers. The chill of religious indifference, hostility to the church and a lack of faith might prevail outside in the modern world. But within, papalism and Marianism disseminated the warmth of home: emotional security through popular piety of every kind, from pilgrimages through devotions for the masses to the celebrations in May when Mary is honoured with candles and flowers.

Here the foundations were laid for what Karl Gabriel has called a 'specifically Catholic social form'. The Catholics of the second half of the nineteenth century and the first half of the twentieth seemed bound up in a closed confessional milieu with its own view of the world. They hardly noticed how bureaucratized and centralized the church's structure of ministry was. The forms of church organization became modernized and sacralized at the same time, and the clergy became more disciplined than ever before because it had been separated from the 'world' as far as possible. The result was an ideologically closed system which legitimated, on the one hand, a distance from the modern world and, on the other, the claim to have a monopoly of ultimate interpretations of the world.

Much contributed to the building up of this anti-modern system and its claim to truth. In parallel with neo-Romanticism, the neo-Gothic in architecture and the neo-Gregorian in music, neo-scholasticism was propagated in the Roman Catholic Church. The church prescribed Neo-Thomism as the normal Roman Catholic theology for all church schools, although this no longer attracted general interest or posed the right theological questions. Theological renewal movements, particularly in the state faculties of Germany, felt the repression of the Curia: the church suppressed whole faculties (Marburg, Giessen) or divided them (Tübingen) and dismissed a whole series of professors, some of whom were even put on the Index (Bonn, Vienna).

The time-lag between developments in the church and in modern society was striking: in the very decade that Charles Darwin announced his theory of evolution to the public, Pius IX for the first time had the idea, as a demonstration of his own fullness of power and *de facto* infallibility, of promulgating a dogma entirely by himself. To promulgate a dogma is an action which traditionally has always been taken at a council in a situation of conflict to ward off heresy. Pius IX's intention was to further traditional piety and to reinforce the Roman system. The strange dogma that he had in mind was that of the 'Immaculate Conception of Mary' (Mary conceived in her mother's body without original sin), dated 1854. We do not find a word in the Bible and in the Catholic tradition of the first millennium about this, and it hardly makes any sense in the light of the theory of evolution.

The opposing forces in Germany and Austria were still strong, especially in the theological centres of Tübingen, Vienna and Munich, although the pope tried to isolate the reform theologians and restrict the bishops with a whole series of doctrinal documents and the deliberate intervention of the papal nuncios. Ten years after Pius IX's dogma, in 1864, a congress of Catholic scholars took place in Munich under the leadership of Germany's most prominent church historian, Ignaz von Döllinger. In response to it the pope published an utterly reactionary encyclical (*Quanta cura*), accompanied by a *Syllabus errorum modernorum*, a *Syllabus of Modern Errors* – eighty in number. All in all, this was an uncompromising defence of the doctrinal and power structure of the Middle Ages and the Counter-Reformation and at the same time a general declaration of war on modernity.

What was pernicious was not that the pope opposed the threat of the omnipotence of the state and the political substitute religions, but that he rejected modern thought as such. Clerical associations and Bible societies were condemned; human rights generally were condemned, as was freedom of conscience, religion and the press, along with civil marriage. Pantheism, naturalism and rationalism, indifferentism and latitudinarianism, socialism and communism were all condemned without any differentiation between them. Any renunciation of the church state was included as an error in the list, which came to a climax in the general condemnation of the statement that the Roman pontifex can and must 'be reconciled and agree with progress, with liberalism and with the new civilization'.

After the emigration of the Reformers and then the modern natural scientists and philosophers, now an emigration of many workers and intellectuals from the Catholic Church had become virtually unavoidable. At the level of science and education, so fundamental to modern men and women, this Catholicism had no more to offer; generally speaking it corresponded to the level of education of the Catholic masses.

One important symptom of this pernicious development was that now a large number of the representative spirits of European modernity had been put on the Index of books forbidden to Catholics. Alongside numerous theologians and critics of the church and Copernicus and Galileo, the founders of modern science, stood the fathers of modern philosophy, Descartes and Pascal, Bayle, Malebranche and Spinoza, together with the British empiricists Hobbes, Locke and Hume. There was also Kant's *Critique of Pure Reason*, of course Rousseau and Voltaire, and later John Stuart Mill, Comte, and also the great historians Gibbon, Condorcet, Ranke, Taine and Gregorovius. Then came Diderot and d'Alembert with their *Encyclopédie* and the *Larousse Dictionary*; Grotius, the constitutional and international jurist, von Pufendorf and de Montesquieu; and finally an elite of modern literature: Heine and Lenau, Hugo, Lamartine, Dumas father and son, Balzac, Flaubert, Zola, Leopardei and d'Annunzio – in our days, Sartre and Simone de Beauvoir, Malaparte, Gide and Kazantzakis ... This 'magisterium' and the 'good Catholic' did not seriously enter into a critical and constructive discussion with modern atheism and secularism; to defend itself, the magisterium made use of apologetic clichés, caricatures and condemnations.

All this showed how much, in Rome, the Roman Catholic paradigm of the Middle Ages had gone on the defensive all along the line. But the modern world, which had largely come into being without, and against, Rome, went its way, little impressed by the backward-looking utopia of a church-state bureaucracy which, pining for the Middle Ages, was generally hostile to reform. Above all, the church called for closed ranks (*acies ordinata*), submission, humility and obedience. But the more that false judgements undermined the Roman 'magisterium' in matters of natural science and biblical exegesis, democracy and public morality, and the more the opposition grew, the more the man in the Vatican was fixated on his own infallibility in order to confirm and legitimate himself. What was once a Counter-Reformation was now a Counter-Enlightenment.

Moreover, three hundred years after the Council of Trent – very much along the lines of this Counter-Enlightenment – a new 'ecumenical council' was convened in Rome in 1869, in the Vatican itself. The majority of the council fathers (many of whom travelled specially from the traditional strongholds of Italy and Spain to lend their support to the council) were stamped by the restoration and romanticism of their early years (politically already superseded since 1848). They were full of fear of liberalism, socialism and rationalistic positivism, and were obsessed with the 'Roman question': whether the papal state, already shrivelled down to Rome and its surroundings as a result of the intervention of the Piedmont government in 1860, was to be given up. In the Curia, people thought that only the solemn definition of papal primacy and infallibility by the ecumenical council could deter the Italian nation from conquering it. The Vatican Council was to be a clear counterpoint to the Council of Constance (1414–18), so that the latter's traditional view of the supremacy of the council over the pope could be forgotten.

And so Pius IX, who had rapidly changed from liberal reformer to political and theological reactionary and enemy of human rights, supported by the Ultramontane preaching and press, especially of France, advanced the definition of the papal prerogatives as his prime personal concern. In the papal pilgrimages and papal audiences which were now becoming customary, and on his many journeys through Italy, the friendly and eloquent man played the role of the one 'persecuted by unchristian powers' and created a favourable mood for a definition of infallibility among the Catholic people and clergy. The Ultramontane indoctrination of the Catholic masses and the administrative centralization of the church apparatus had meanwhile made progress, not least through the growing Roman influence on the election of bishops and the internal concerns of the dioceses generally. This influence was exercised by bestowing the title of prelate and honours on clergy and laity who were well-disposed towards Rome, by nominating suitable cardinals and soon also by establishing Roman places of education for candidates for the priesthood from all over the world (on the model of the Collegium Germanicum).

However, many bishops knew the other side of the jovial pope, this dangerously emotional man with a superficial theological education, unfamiliar with modern scientific methods, egocentric and surrounded by narrow-minded advisers. There was plenty of opposition at the Vatican Council. And bishops with a broad education like the Bishop of Orleans, Felix Dupanloup, and especially the Bishop of Rottenburg, Karl Joseph Hefele, who as Tübingen Professor of Church History had written a history of the councils in many volumes, knew what counter-arguments church history had against papal infallibility.

Despite all the opposition in the episcopate, after weeks of vigorous controversies, and at the energetic urging of the pope, who rejected all objections and compromise proposals, two papal dogmas were defined on 18 July 1870. Before they were passed, not only the archbishops of Milan and St Louis, Missouri, but also the representatives of the most important metropolitan sees of France, Germany and Austro-Hungary departed. To the present day the following decrees are the object of resolute Orthodox and Protestant repudiation, and the cause of a split within the Catholic Church which could easily have been avoided:

• The pope has a legally binding primacy of jurisdiction over every single national church and every individual Christian.

• The pope possesses the gift of infallibility in his own solemn magisterial decisions. These solemn (*ex cathedra*) decisions are infallible on the basis of special support from the Holy Spirit and are immutable (irreformable) intrinsically, not by virtue of the assent of the church.

The pope himself saw the controversy over the church state as a further act in the battle in world history between God and Satan, which in a completely irrational trust in the victory of Divine Providence he hoped to win. But the infallibility pope erred: he lost the battle over the papal state. Exactly two months after the definition of infallibility, on 20 September 1870, Italian troops marched into Rome. A popular vote by the Romans resulted in an overwhelming majority against the pope. The Vatican Council, which was broken off because of the Franco-Prussian War, was not to be continued.

In the episcopate the resistance to the dogma of infallibility soon collapsed: Bishop Hefele was the last to bow. Yet in

Germany in 1870–1 there were numerous protest meetings and pamphlets, and Catholic congresses in Munich and Cologne. Here the Catholic Enlightenment (whose spokesman was Ignaz Heinrich von Weissenberg, several times rejected for the epis-copate by the reactionary Leo XII) had already done much work towards a reform of clerical education, worship and hymns in the vernacular, episcopal independence and the abolition of compulsory celibacy. Out of the protests was formed (under the spiritual leadership of Döllinger) the Old Catholic Church (in Switzerland the Christian Catholic Church): this is a church which continues to be Catholic but is 'Rome-free'. With validly consecrated bishops, it seeks to hold to the faith of the church of the first millennium (the first seven councils), to implement a synodical-episcopal constitution with great autonomy for the local church, and accord the pope no more than a 'primacy of honour'. Customs introduced in the Middle Ages, or not until the nineteenth century, like compulsory celibacy, the obligation to go to confession once a year, the cult of relics, the rosary, veneration of the heart of Jesus and the heart of Mary, are repudiated. In many respects this little, bold and ecumenically open Old Catholic Church from the beginning anticipated reforms of the Second Vatican Council and recently has even gone beyond them with the ordination of women.

Of course in papal Rome at the time of the First Vatican Council things were seen differently: after all, in 1870 the Roman system, which had endured since the eleventh century despite all resistance, revolution and interruptions, had finally and at long last found its cornerstone. It was thought that the pope, now an absolute ruler with infallible teaching, would in future easily be able to solve all problems and make all necessary decisions. However, when faced with these two papal dogmas, not only Old Catholics were asking what had become of the message of Jesus of Nazareth in the second millennium. Or, to put it quite pointedly: What would Jesus himself, to whom this pope appealed with his council, have said about them? I do not know how seriously Karl Rahner, the theologian of the Second Vatican Council, wanted his criticism to be taken when he remarked: 'Jesus would not have understood any of it!'

VIII   The Catholic Church – Present and
Future

Would the pope still be the pope, as understood by Roman ideology, if he abandoned the idea of infallibility? The status of the papal state was discussed in the same way in the nineteenth century. For a thousand years it was impossible to imagine the papacy without a great papal state. But with the creation of the Italian nation-state, the papacy was forced to be content with a pro-forma state: a dwarf state around St Peter's with a summer seat at Castel Gondolfo and a few extra-territorial buildings and bits of property, all in all barely a quarter of the size of the Principality of Monaco, with less than five hundred inhabitants. It is understandable that after the Italian conquest of Rome, for decades the popes initially played the role of 'prisoner of the Vatican' and aroused much sympathy, although it was in fact only their own dogma of *non possumus*, 'we cannot', which prevented them from leaving the Vatican and thus, by doing so, accepting the new situation between church and state.

Yet now, even without a papal state, the popes were effectively able to bring to bear in the Catholic Church the papal sole rule promised by the First Vatican Council – at the cost of the traditional independence of the local churches and their bishops and the age-old synodical elements. On the other hand, the popes had made a substantial contribution to the Catholic Church by keeping its structural unity and international Catholicity in a time of nationalism; indeed, after a period of revolution they had even been able to strengthen their role in the world.

The successor to the infallibility pope, Leo XIII (1878–1903), wisely did not lay claim to infallibility and was concerned for a reconciliation of church and culture. He opened up the Catholic Church to social and political developments. He ended not only the *Kulturkampf* with the German empire which broke out over the Protestant reaction to the *Syllabus of Modern Errors* and the definition of infallibility, but also similar political conflicts with Switzerland and Latin American states. Although he maintained the need for a church state and the papal dogmas, Leo XIII corrected Rome's negative attitude to modernity, to democracy and liberal freedoms, in part even to modern exegesis and church history, and above all to the 'social question'. Now that the pope was no longer responsible for the socially retrograde church state, he could publish the already long overdue social encyclical *Rerum novarum* (1891), almost half a century after the Communist Manifesto. Contrary to nineteenth-century *laissez-faire* liberalism, the pope endorsed regulatory interventions by the state, and contrary to socialism he affirmed private property. Many 'Reform Catholics' now hoped that there would be a fundamental change in Rome. But they would be disappointed. Towards the end of Leo's pontificate retrogressive tendencies again became visible, for example in the foundation of a Papal Biblical Commission to supervise exegetes. The skilful combination of absolutism within the church with simultaneous social (and sometimes populist) initiatives would, with changing tactical emphases, continue to remain Rome's strategy down to the present pontificate.

Leo's successor Pius X (1903–14), for many years a pastor and diocesan bishop, certainly devoted himself intensively to renewal within the church, to better seminary education and a celebration of the eucharist at which communion is received regularly. He also reorganized the Roman Curia. But none of these reforms was far-reaching. In foreign policy, too, the tenth Pius fell into line with the other nine, rejected all democratic and parliamentarian tendencies and allowed political and diplomatic ties to be broken off with France and Spain. In Italy he enacted measures against the Christian Democrats, and in Germany he took a stand in favour of Catholic workers' associations against the Christian trade unions.

Even worse, Pius X suppressed any reconciliation of Catholic teaching with modern science and knowledge. Under the disparaging label 'modernism' he led an anti-modern cleansing action on a grand scale, a formal heresy-hunt against all reform theologians, especially exegetes and historians. In France, Germany, North America and Italy, proceedings were taken against the Catholic intellectual elite, with sanctions of various kinds (the Index, excommunication, dismissal). A new *Syllabus of Modern Errors* and an anti-modern encyclical (1907), indeed an 'anti-modernist oath' (1910, many pages in length), imposed on all the clergy, was meant to eradicate the modernists once and for all. The same was true of the dogmatic decrees of the Biblical Commission on every possible question of biblical history. Pius was helped to spy on bishops, theologians and politicians by a curial secret organization (Sodalitium Pianum), comparable to today's Opus Dei, which, under the leadership of the Vatican under-secretary of state Umberto Benigni, was able to institute what Josef Schmidlin has called 'a pernicious subsidiary government of the church'. 'If Pius himself is not guilty of being the chief author of this pernicious world plot, at least he is an accomplice in it, because he systematically urged it on and protectively held his rigid hand over it.' The extent to which Roman beatifications have meanwhile degenerated in our day to gestures in church politics is shown by the canonization of this very pope by Pius XIII in 1954. The fact that, even more recently, the Vatican has opened the archive of the Inquisition only up to 1903, to the accession of Pius X, shows how fearful people there are of the truth.

Even in the college of cardinals, many people were discontented with the reactionary and inquisitorial course of Pius X. This was shown by the election as pope of Giacoma della Chiesa, the very man whom Pius excluded from being undersecretary of state by nominating him Archbishop of Bologna, and whom he nominated cardinal only immediately before his death. As Benedict XV (1914–22), the new pope put a speedy end to Benigni's secret organization, which was poisoning everything (Benigni became an agent of Mussolini). This pope was intensively involved in mediation in the First World War, but without success, and on all sides continued the conciliatory policy of Leo XIII. Still, in the middle of the war (1917) he approved the new *Codex Iuris Canonici* (code of canon law) already prepared under his predecessor – with no consent from the world episcopate. The universal primacy of law defined by Vatican I, and the centralist system bound up with it, were thus given a legal blessing and safeguard in every detail; for example, contrary to early Catholic tradition, the right of the pope to nominate all bishops was postulated.

The global catastrophe of the First World War (1914–18) made it abundantly clear to all those with eyes to see that the leading values of modernity were in crisis: the modern absolutizing of reason, progress, the nation and industry was shattered. Belief in reason and progress, nationalism, capitalism and socialism had failed. But the opportunity for a new, peaceful, more just world order in 1918 – the concrete proposals of the American President Woodrow Wilson – was lost by the European practitioners of *realpolitik*. And Europe had to pay dearly for that with the reactionary movements of Fascism, Nazism and Communism, which in a 'modern' way idealized race or class and their 'leaders' and got in the way of a new and better world order. However, the First World War set in motion the global revolution which would become manifest after the Second World War: the change from the Eurocentric paradigm of modernity, which had a colonialist, imperialist and capitalist stamp, to the truly global, polycentric paradigm of post-modernity, which had an ecumenical orientation. However, this in particular was only partly recognized in Rome, and then too late.

Benedict's learned successor Pius XI (1922–39) ruled in a similarly autocratic way and propagated the 'extension of the kingdom of God', above all through the 'Catholic Action' of the laity, though they were to remain an extension of the arm of the hierarchy. He encouraged the indigenous clergy in the missions, and, in Rome, church learning and art. In an anti-ecumenical encyclical (*Mortalium animos*, 1928), however, he gave extensive reasons why Catholics were forbidden to take part in the great Lausanne ecumenical conference held by Faith and Order, a predecessor of the World Council of Churches in 1929. And in reaction to the Anglican Lambeth Conference, with no opposition from the episcopate, in 1930 he fixed the Catholic Church on its pernicious course against birth control (the encyclical *Casti connubii*). This was later a chief argument for the 'infallible' consensus of pope and bishops in this doctrine. The same year he elevated to the status of 'teacher of the church' Robert Bellarmine, SJ (died 1621), who in his short catechism answered the question 'Who is a Christian?' in a good curial way: 'One who obeys the pope and the pastor appointed by him.'

However, it is to Pius XI that the Catholic Church owes the new social encyclical *Quadragesimo anno* (1931). Taking up

Rerum novarum, it states the need for reforms by the application of the principle of subsidiarity, i.e., that decisions are taken at the lowest possible level, but at the same time develops the pre-modern leading value of an 'order based on class distinction'. It is to the same pope that the Catholic Church owes above all the solution to the 'Roman question'. Confronted with the Fascist Duce Benito Mussolini, after almost sixty years he made the *non possumus*, which had prevented the popes from leaving the Vatican and recognizing the new situation, into a *possumus*, 'We can'. In the Lateran Treaties of 1929 the pope was recognized by the Italian state as sovereign of the little papal state and compensated for loss of all future rights with a gigantic sum of money.

In order to safeguard the position of the Catholic Church in countries concerned in the turbulent period between the wars and at the same time to establish the centralist church system, the Vatican now concluded many concordats, among them those with the Fascist regimes of Spain and Portugal, a dubious enterprise. The *Reichskonkordat* which Secretary of State Pacelli negotiated with Hitler's Germany was to prove fatal – an endorsement of Hitler which was unprecedented at that time. Certainly Pius XI himself was a resolute opponent of the Nazis and refused to receive Hitler in the Vatican. He condemned National Socialist doctrine, politics and the violation of the concordat in his German-language encyclical *Mit brennender Sorge* (With burning concern) of 1937. An encyclical against racism and anti-Semitism was also in preparation, but Pius XI died a few months before the outbreak of the Second World War. His successor was that selfsame Secretary of State Eugenio Pacelli who was able to negotiate an apparently shrewd concordat with Hitler. The encyclical against racism and anti-Semitism was pigeonholed. I must emphasize something else about this Pope Pius XII, who is still the subject of vigorous controversy today.

Silence about the Holocaust

That in his confession of guilt in 2000 John Paul II was still silent about the mistakes of his papal predecessors is doubtless connected with the papal claim to 'infallibility', although, as we saw, these predecessors bear most of the blame for the schism between West and East and the Reformation, for the Crusades and the Inquisition, for the persecutions of heretics and the burning of witches. What is most incomprehensible of all is his failure to mention Pius XII's silence over the Holocaust. Despite all his lamentations about the persecution of Jews and anti-Semitism 'through Christians wherever and whenever', even in the Holocaust Memorial Yad Vashem in March 2000 the pope did not utter a word about the institutional church, the Vatican and Pius XII. Rather, he wanted to beatify this pope like his predecessor, Pius IX, who ruthlessly took measures against the Jews, restricted their freedoms, in 1850 even had the walls of the Jewish ghetto in Rome rebuilt, and in Bologna in 1858 allowed the six-year-old Jewish child Edgaro Mortara to be snatched from his parents by the papal police because he had been given secret Catholic baptism by a maid when he was ill. The child was abducted to Rome, and despite worldwide protests (including the intervention of Napoleon III and the Emperor Franz Joseph) was inexorably given a Catholic upbringing. Indeed, years later he was even ordained priest. It was only after the invasion of the Italian armies of liberation that the walls of the Roman ghetto could finally fall, but the de-ghettoizing of the Jews was followed by the self-ghettoizing of the papacy.

Time and again it has been asked why it is that this selfsame hierocratic Pius XII (1939–58) – the last unassailed representative of the medieval Counter-Reformation anti-modernist paradigm, who even after the Second World War (1950) proceeded extremely forcefully along the lines of Pius IX with the definition of a second 'infallible' Marian dogma (the physical assumption of Mary into heaven), banned the French worker priests and sacked all the most important theologians of his time – from the beginning resisted a public condemnation of National Socialism and anti-Semitism.

To understand this, one has to be aware that the actions of this expressly Germanophile church diplomat, with no pastoral experience, who thought above all in legal and diplomatic terms, rather than theologically in the light of the gospel, were fixated on the Curia and the institution instead of pastorally on men and women. Since the shock that Pacelli experienced as a young nuncio in Munich, when witnessing the 'soviet republic' of 1918, obsessed with a fear of physical contact and a fear of communism, his attitude had been deeply authoritarian and anti-democratic ('Führer Catholicism'). So he was almost predisposed to a pragmatic anti-communist alliance with totalitarian Nazism (but also with the Fascist regimes in Italy, Spain and Portugal). This professional diplomat, whose good intentions one cannot deny, was always concerned with the freedom and power of the institutional church (the Curia, the hierarchy, corporations, schools, associations, pastoral letters, the free practice of religion): 'human rights' and 'democracy' remained alien to him all his life.

As for the Jews, for Pacelli, as a Roman, Rome and Rome again and again was the new Zion, the centre of the church and of the world. He never showed any personal sympathy whatsoever for the Jews; rather, he saw them as the people who murdered God. As the triumphalist representative of a Rome ideology, he saw Christ as a Roman and Jerusalem as replaced by Rome. Thus from the beginning, like the whole of the Roman Curia he was against the foundation of a Jewish state in Palestine.

Certainly National Socialism and Judaism presented this monarch of the church, who impressed the whole world, with a conflict of conscience. But it should not be forgotten that as early as 1931 Pacelli pressurized the Catholic German Chancellor Brüning into a coalition with the National Socialists and broke with Brüning when he refused. Moreover, as early as 20 July 1933, Pacelli unnecessarily concluded that baneful *Reichskonkordat* with the Nazi regime: this was the first international treaty with the 'Führer', who had come to power only a few months beforehand, and it bestowed on Hitler recognition in foreign politics; in domestic politics it integrated the Catholics and their rebellious episcopate and clergy into the Nazi system. Like some others in the Curia, Pacelli was aware of the affinity between his own authoritarian, i.e., anti-Protestant, anti-liberal, anti-socialist, anti-modern understanding of the church, and an authoritarian Fascist and Nazi understanding of the state: here were 'unity', 'order', 'discipline' and the 'Führer principle' at the level of the natural state, just as they were there at the level of the supernatural church.

In any case, excessively overestimating the importance of diplomacy and concordats, Pacelli fundamentally had only two political aims: the battle against Communism and the battle for the preservation of the institutional church. The wretched Jewish question was an insignificant matter for him. Certainly, unlike many in the West, he was not deceived about Stalin. And certainly, as pope, especially towards the end of the war, he worked hard with diplomatic approaches and charitable help to save individual Jews or groups of Jews, particularly in Italy and Rome. In two addresses, in 1942 and 1943, he briefly, and in general and abstract terms, lamented the fate of the 'unfortunate people' who were being persecuted for their race. But this pope never used the word 'Jew' in public, just as the anti-Nazi encyclical *Mit brennender Sorge* of 1937, for which he was also partly responsible, did not once mention the word 'Jew' or race. And just as Pacelli did not protest against the Nuremberg race laws (1935) and the pogrom of *Kristallnacht* (1938), so too he did not protest against the Italian attack on Ethiopia and Albania (on Good Friday 1939) and, finally, did not protest against the unleashing of the Second World War by the Nazis in their attack on Poland on 1 September 1939.

Would a protest have been useless? Konrad Adenauer, who later became chancellor, at any rate thought quite differently. The public protest of a single German bishop (Galen of Munster in 1941) against Hitler's monstrous 'euthanasia programme' had already proved (although the Conference of Bishops was silent) to have a wide public effect, and the Lutheran bishops of Denmark were quite successful in their public support for the Jews. But Pius XII left the Catholic bishops of the Netherlands, who similarly supported the Jews, in the lurch. This man, who in other respects spoke on every possible theme in thousands of addresses, avoided any public protest against anti-Semitism, even the cancellation of the concordat, which the Nazis had constantly failed to observe from the beginning. The man who, after the war, would excommunicate all members of the Communist Party throughout the world because of the domestic political situation in Italy had not the slightest thought of excommunicating the 'Catholics' Hitler, Himmler, Goebbels and Bormann (Göring, Eichmann and others were nominally Protestants). Pius was silent about the notorious German war crimes all over Europe; indeed, even though from 1942 he was extremely well informed by the nuncio in Bern and Italian army chaplains in Russia, and was even raged at by his German confidante Sister Pasqualina, he was silent about the Holocaust, the greatest mass murder of all times.

This silence about the Holocaust was more than a political failure; it was a moral failure. It was a refusal to make a moral protest regardless of political opportunities; a refusal, moreover, by a Christian who thought that he deserved to bear the title (though this has been customary only since the Middle Ages) as 'representative (not only of Peter but) of Christ' and who suppressed his mistakes after the war, restrained deviants within Catholicism with authoritarian measures, and up to his death refused diplomatic recognition to the young democratic state of Israel. The subtitle of Rolf Hochhuth's play about Pius XII, *The Representative*, 'A Christian Tragedy', is not inappropriate.

But to beatify Pius XII, like beatifying Pius IX – the enemy of Jews, Protestants, human rights, the freedom of religion, modern culture – would be a Vatican farce and a disavowal of the most recent papal confessions of guilt. 'No, he is not a saint,' we were told in the Collegium Germanicum by his loyal private secretary Father Robert Leiber, SJ, even in the pope's lifetime. 'No, he is not a saint, but a man of the church.' 'But what lies behind the wish of a pope to canonize other popes?' the international journal *Concilium* asked in a statement issued in July 2000. 'Is this campaign aimed at reinforcing papal authority or is it to be understood as an attempt to misuse the important act of recognizing holiness to safeguard ideological aims?'

We owe it to another pope that the situation of the papacy in respect of Judaism does not look quite so wretched. This pope is Angelo Giuseppe Roncalli, elected Pius's successor on 28

October 1958 as John XXIII. Regarded at seventy-seven as a 'transitional' pope, he became the pope of a revolutionary transition which released the Catholic Church from its internal rigidity.

The most significant pope of the twentieth century

It was John XXIII (1958–63) and no one else who, in a pontificate of barely five years, ushered in a new era in the history of the Catholic Church. Against massive resistance from the Curia, with considerable historical learning and pastoral experience, he opened up to the church, immured in a medieval Counter-Reformation anti-modern paradigm, the way to renewal (aggiornamento), to a proclamation of the gospel in keeping with the time; to an understanding with the other Christian churches, with Judaism and the other world religions; to contacts with the Eastern states; to international social justice (the encyclical *Mater et magistra*, 1961); and to openness to the modern world generally and the affirmation of human rights (the encyclical *Pacem in terris*, 1963). Through his collegial behaviour he strengthened the role of the bishops. In all this, Pope John showed a new pastoral understanding of the papal office.

Roncalli's new attitude to Judaism, which was in sharp contrast to that of Pacelli, must also be said to be historic. During the Second World War, as apostolic delegate in Turkey, he had saved the lives of thousands of Jews from Romania and Bulgaria, especially children (by issuing blank baptismal certificates). Made pope in 1958, the very next year he did something which his predecessor had always refused to do: in the intercessions of the Good Friday liturgy he deleted the phrase the 'treacherous

Jews' in a traditional prayer (*pro perfidis Judaeis*) in favour of intercessions which were friendly to the Jews. For the first time he received a group of more than one hundred American Jews and greeted them with the words of the biblical Joseph in Egypt, 'I am Joseph, your brother!' And one day he spontaneously had his car stop at the synagogue in Rome so that he could bless the Jews who happened to be streaming out. On the night before the death of this Pope, Rome's chief rabbi went with numerous Jewish faithful to pray with the Catholics.

But John XXIII's historically most significant act was the announcement of the Second Vatican Council on 25 January 1959, which surprised the whole world. He solemnly opened the council on 11 October 1962. This corrected Pius XII – apart from his pioneering encyclical on Catholic biblical exegesis (*Divino afflante Spiritu*, 1943) – on almost all decisive points: reform of the liturgy, ecumenism, anti-Communism, freedom of religion, the 'modern world' and above all the attitude to Judaism. Encouraged by the new Pope, at last the bishops once again displayed self-confidence and felt that they were a college with their own 'apostolic' authority.

Against vehement opposition from the traditionally anti-Jewish Curia, towards the end of the council the declaration *Nostra aetate*, about the religions of the world, was passed. For the first time in a council, a 'collective guilt' of the Jewish people, then or even now for the death of Jesus, was strictly disavowed; any rejection or cursing of the old people of God was opposed, indeed 'all outbreaks of hatred, persecutions and manifestations of anti-Semitism which have been directed against the Jews at any time by anyone' were lamented, and 'mutual knowledge and respect' were promised. Here the council finally did justice to the intentions of John XXIII.

*

An overall assessment of the Second Vatican Council (1962–5) is by no means easy. But as one who witnessed the council at the time and has criticisms of it today, almost four decades after its conclusion, I maintain my overall verdict: for the Catholic Church, this council represented an irrevocable turning-point. With the Second Vatican Council, the Catholic Church – despite all the difficulties and hindrances posed by the medieval Roman system – attempted to implement two paradigm changes at once: it integrated fundamental features of both the Reformation paradigm and the paradigm of the Enlightenment and modernity.

First of all, it integrated the Reformation paradigm. Catholic complicity in the split in the church was recognized, as was the need for constant reform. *Ecclesia semper reformanda*, constant renewal of the church in life and teaching according to the gospel, was now also the official Catholic view. The other Christian fellowships were finally recognized as churches. An ecumenical attitude was called for from the whole Catholic Church. At the same time, a series of central concerns of the gospel were taken up at least in principle and often also in practical terms: there was a new respect for the Bible in worship, theology and church life, as in the life of individual believers generally. There was authentic worship for the people in the vernacular and a reformed celebration of the eucharist related to the community. There was a revaluation of the laity through parish and diocesan councils and the admission of them to the study of theology. The church was adapted to national and local conditions by an emphasis on the local church and the national conferences of bishops. Finally, there was a reform of popular piety and an abolition of many special forms of piety from the Middle Ages, the baroque period and the nineteenth century.

There was also an integration of the modern paradigm. Here

are a few central key tenets. There was a clear affirmation of freedom of religion and conscience and of human rights generally, which had been condemned by Pius XII in 1953. There was a fundamental acknowledgement of complicity in anti-Semitism and a positive turn towards Judaism, from which Christianity derives. But there was also a new, constructive attitude towards Islam and the other world religions. It was recognized that in principle salvation is also possible outside Christianity, even for atheists and agnostics, if they act in accordance with their conscience. There was a fundamentally positive attitude to modern progress, too, which had long been ostracized, and to the secular world, science and democracy generally.

When it came to the understanding of the church in particular, the council's Constitution on the Church clearly dissociated itself from the understanding of the church as a kind of supernatural Roman empire which had been held since the eleventh century. In this view the pope stands at the head as absolute sole ruler; then comes the 'aristocracy' of the bishops and priests; and finally, in a passive function, the 'subject people' of the faithful. There was a desire to overcome such a clericalized, legalistic and triumphalist picture of the church, which was vigorously criticized at the council. Therefore the first version of the Constitution on the Church, produced by the curial preparatory commission, was rejected by the council itself in a dramatic vote, by an overwhelming majority. The decisive change which had finally been carried through was that all statements about the church hierarchy were prefaced by a section about the people of God. 'People of God' is understood as a fellowship of faith which is constantly on the way in the world, a sinful and provisional pilgrim folk, ready for ever new reform.

At the same time, truths which had been ignored for centuries were recalled. Those who hold office do not stand over the people of God but are within it; they are not rulers but servants. The universal priesthood of believers is to be taken as seriously as the significance of local churches in the framework of the church as a whole: as worshipping communities, they are the church in a quite original sense. And the bishops, regardless of the papal primacy, are to exercise a communal, collegial responsibility for leading the whole church. For the bishop becomes bishop not through nomination by the pope but through consecration. Finally, the diaconate was revived (though up to the present only for males) and the law of celibacy was abolished at least for deacons. However, all this was only one aspect of the council. There was another, less positive aspect.

From the beginning, the machinery of the Curia did all it could to keep the council under control. It was quickly understood that in contrast to Vatican I, Vatican II had a solid progressive majority. However, from the start the Curia ensured (a fatal concession by Pope John) that the presidents of the individual council commissions were cardinals of the Curia and that both the general secretary and the secretaries of the commissions were Curia theologians. It was as if, in a parliament, the parliamentary committees of investigation were completely controlled by the controlling ministers themselves and their helpers.

The result was constant wrangling between the council and the Curia. Time and again the progressive conciliar majority sought to compromise with the tiny reactionary minority and the curial apparatus which supported it. Time and again also the majority at the council was overruled by individual decisions of the pope or changes to the text made by the pope himself (as happened over the Decree on Ecumenism). No bishop, no conference of bishops, ventured a protest.

Sadly, John XXIII died after the first session of the council, at the age of eighty-two, but all too early. If the Pius popes do not deserve beatification, John XXIII does not need it: the Catholic people have already long beatified him without dubious proofs from miracles. Roncalli was replaced by the Montini pope, Paul VI (1967–78), serious but wavering (like Hamlet), who ultimately, because of his whole career, thought in curial rather than conciliar terms.

Certainly, in some cases, above all in matters of the freedom of religion and Judaism, the majority at the council could even now oppose the Curia, because ultimately this was also the will of the pope. But specifically with respect to the church constitution and a correction of the First Vatican Council, there was a momentous compromise. Roughly speaking, it looked like this. The Curia tolerated the first two basic chapters of the Vatican II Constitution on the Church which speak of the church as 'mystery' and of 'people of God' and have a biblical orientation. But in the third chapter it clearly re-established the old hierarchical structure – with some expansions on collegiality, the consecration of bishops and infallibility (the ominous Article 25 took over from the Roman theological textbooks, without any discussion, the thesis of an 'ordinary' infallible magisterium even of the bishops). All this was finally sealed with a *Nota praevia explicativa* by Paul VI, forced on the council: with an appeal to his allegedly 'higher authority', at the end of the third session he put in the middle of the text of the constitution the old ideology of primacy as a hermeneutical rule. This prejudiced everything. There was scandal, sorrow, anger and indignation among the bishops, but no protest about this or resistance to it and other arbitrary acts of the pope, which again put the episcopal collegiality out of joint.

The Roman system, which broke through in the eleventh century with Gregorian Rome and attributed sole rule over the church to the pope and his Curia, was shaken but not done away with by the Second Vatican Council, just as had happened once before at the Council of Constance. It was now tacitly accepted that the Roman system of government was strictly rejected by the Orthodox churches of the East as by the churches of the Reformation, but that they would probably have few objections to a real ecumenical papacy.

Two of the three central practical demands of the Reformers were met in principle: the use of the vernacular in the liturgy and the opening up of eucharistic communion to include offering the chalice to the laity as well. But other council taboos were to prove baneful. The marriage of priests could not even be discussed. Nor could there be discussion of the practical demands of the Reformers, divorce, a new order for the nomination of bishops, reform of the Curia or, above all, the papacy itself. On one and the same afternoon three speeches were made by important cardinals in favour of an understanding doctrine of birth control (contraception). But the discussion was immediately stopped by the pope, and the matter (like the question of confessionally mixed marriages) was referred to a papal commission. This would later decide against the traditional Roman teaching but was overruled by the pope himself in 1968 with the encyclical *Humanae vitae*.

At the council it was impossible to achieve more than a compromise between the medieval Counter-Reformation anti-modernist paradigm of the church and a contemporary paradigm. Therefore, during the course of the council (and this too is part of this history), I decided to develop a responsible understanding of the church for the present time which was consistently based on the biblical message, and wrote my book *The Church*. In the very year of its publication, 1967, Inquisition proceedings were opened by the Holy Office (Congregation for the Doctrine of Faith): all translations were immediately forbidden, a decree which I ignored (the English edition appeared in 1968). Negotiations lasting for years began on the fair conditions for a 'colloquium'. What is now taken for granted in any secular court – inspection of the record, the involvement of a defender and the possibility of appeal to an independent authority – is never allowed in the Roman proceedings. If the accused does not immediately submit, he is in fact already condemned. Meanwhile, however, further dramatic developments had been taking place within the post-conciliar church which many Catholics looked upon with suspicion. People in general had begun to ask where the Catholic Church was going.

Restoration instead of renewal

Almost immediately after the conclusion of the Second Vatican Council it was obvious that, despite concessions over the reform of the liturgy, the renewal of the Catholic Church and ecumenical understanding with the other Christian churches wanted by John XXIII, the council had got stuck. At the same time, the church hierarchy was beginning to lose credibility to a dramatic extent. That Roman dissociation of 'foreign policy' from 'domestic policy' which is now typical was already evident in 1967: outwardly (where it cost the church nothing), the church was progressive, as in the encyclical *Populorum progressio*. But inwardly, in its own concerns, the church was reactionary and published an encyclical on celibacy (*Sacerdotalis coelibatus*): the highest truths of the gospel were marshalled to prove what cannot be proved; that there must be compulsory celibacy for priests. This document too did nothing to remove the basic contradiction: calling upon that same gospel, the leaders of the Roman Catholic Church twisted what, according to the gospel, was a completely free vocation to celibacy into a law which oppressed freedom.

Here, for the first time since the council, the pope, again in a pre-conciliar, authoritarian way, made a unilateral decision, completely scorning the collegiality of the bishops which was solemnly resolved on by the council. This decision on celibacy was particularly important for the churches in Latin America, Africa and Asia where there is a dearth of priests, yet the pope himself forbade discussion of it at the council. Again there was no storm of protest from the episcopate which, for the first time since the council, had openly been snubbed; only a diminishing number of bishops in Belgium and Canada raised their voices in favour of collegiality.

It was quite evident that, despite the impulse of the council, in this post-conciliar period it had not proved possible to bring a decisive change to the authoritarian, institutional and personal power structure of church government in the spirit of the Christian message: despite all the unavoidable changes, pope, Curia and most bishops continued to behave in a pre-conciliar, authoritarian way. Little seemed to have been learned from the conciliar process. In Rome and in other areas of the church, personalities still held the reins of power who showed more interest in preserving that power and the convenient status quo than in serious renewal in the spirit of the gospel and collegiality.

In every possible decision, small and great, there was still an appeal to the Holy Spirit, to the apostolic authority allegedly given by Christ. The extent of this became clear to all when, in

1968, with a new pernicious encyclical, against contraception, *Humanae vitae*, Paul VI hurled the church into a crisis of credibility which still exists today. Once again, what a time-lag there was between developments in the church and in society: this retrograde encyclical appeared precisely three months after 'May 1968', when in France the great social upheavals were beginning which essentially implied a questioning of all traditional authorities. *Humanae vitae* was the first instance in the history of the church in the twentieth century when the vast majority of people and clergy refused obedience to the pope in an important matter, though in the papal view this was in fact an 'infallible' teaching of the 'ordinary' magisterium of pope and bishops (Article 25 of the Constitution on the Church). This was a precise parallel to the most recent rejection by John Paul II of the ordination of women 'for time and eternity', which is also explicitly declared to be infallible.

This whole development was deeply disturbing. What was the deeper cause of the revival of authoritarianism? It was the Roman will for power and the doctrine of an alleged infallibility of church teaching and papal decisions (which was never investigated after Vatican I). Of course this does not allow former mistakes to be corrected and prevents thoroughgoing reform. That is why my book *Infallible?* had to be written. It appeared as 'An Enquiry', punctually on 18 July 1970, the centenary of the Vatican I declaration on infallibility. I was ready for a storm of criticism from Rome, but not for the broad attack by theologian friends like Karl Rahner, who broke up the unitary front of conciliar reform theology. To the present day Catholic theology has not recovered from this split.

The consequence of all this is that whereas, in 1968, 1360 theologians, men and women from all over the world, happily subscribed to the declaration 'For the Freedom of Theology'

which was produced in Tübingen; numerous Catholic theologians took part in the debate on infallibility at the beginning
of the 1970s with highly critical contributions; and in 1972 we
could still drum up thirty-three well-known Catholic theologians from Europe and North America for the Tübingen declaration 'Against Resignation' which called for the reform of
the Catholic Church; seven years later, after 18 December 1979
and the withdrawal by the church of my permission to teach,
things looked completely different. Since then, hardly a single
Catholic theologian has dared to question outright the doctrine
of infallibility.

Whereas Paul VI still allowed tolerant contradiction (and my
loyal opposition), now – after the death of the thirty-day Pope
John Paul I in circumstances which still have not been clarified –
on 16 October 1978, a quite different pope came to power: the
first non-Italian pope since Hadrian VI, a pope from Poland.

Betrayal of the council

Given the splitting of the world into two power blocks, the
election of Karol Wojtyla a 'pope from the East', was generally
welcomed in the Catholic Church. From the beginning, John
Paul II proved, unlike many statesmen, to be a man of character,
deeply rooted in the Christian faith, an impressive champion of
peace, of human rights, of social justice, and later also of inter-
religious dialogue, but at the same time also the champion of a
strong church. He is a man with charisma, who in an impressive
way, with an impressive gift for publicity, can satisfy the longing
of the masses for a morally trustworthy model of the kind that
has become so rare in contemporary society. Amazingly rapidly
he has become a media superstar, and for many people in the

Catholic Church, he was at first a kind of living cult figure.

But after a year, his course of conservatism and restoration was so clearly recognizable that in every respect he had to be courteously but unambiguously criticized. My article 'A Year of John Paul II', published in the great newspapers of the world on the anniversary of his election, was an 'interim assessment' reminding people of the Second Vatican Council. It proved to be the key document in the withdrawal of my permission to teach in the church precisely two months later. The article attracted public attention far beyond the Catholic Church. Can one make a different assessment a good twenty years after it? In the course of his long pontificate, the positive image of this pope has also changed fundamentally for most Catholics, at least within the developed countries. Today John Paul II appears to them less of a successor to John XXIII than to Pius XII, that pope who, despite the tremendous personality cult which he enjoyed during his lifetime, has left relatively few positive traces in the most recent history of the church.

Certainly the good intentions of this pope too must be recognized, and also his concern for the identity and clarity of the Catholic Church; however, we should not be deceived by well-organized mass meetings and media spectacles staged by specialists. By comparison with the seven fat years of the Catholic Church which coincided with the pontificate of John XXIII and the Second Vatican Council (1958–65), the three times seven years of the Wojtyla pontificate are lean in substance. Despite countless speeches and expensive 'pilgrimages' (with debts running into millions for some local churches), hardly any progress worth taking seriously has been made in the Catholic Church or the ecumenical world.

Although not an Italian, coming from a country where neither the Reformation nor the Enlightenment could become established, John Paul II is very much to the taste of the Curia. In the style of the populist Pius popes, paying great attention to the media, the former Archbishop of Krakow – who in the tricky papal commission on birth control stood out for his constant, politically well-calculated absences – with his charismatic radiance and the acting talent which he has preserved from his youth, gave the Vatican what the White House would soon also possess with Ronald Reagan. Here, too, was the 'great communicator' who, with charm, sportsmanship and symbolic gestures, could present even the most conservative doctrine or practice as acceptable. Priests who applied for laicization were the first to feel the change in climate associated with him, then theologians, and soon also bishops and finally women.

It became increasingly clear, even for admirers, what the real intention of this pope had been from the beginning, despite all verbal assertions: a brake was to be applied to the conciliar movement, reform within the church was to be stopped; real understanding with the Eastern churches, Protestants and Anglicans was to be blocked; and dialogue with the modern world was to be replaced with one-sided teaching and decrees. Looked at more closely, his 're-evangelization' has meant 're-Catholicization' and his wordy 'ecumenism' has, under the surface, been aimed at a 'return' to the Catholic Church.

Granted, John Paul II cites the Second Vatican Council time and again. But the emphasis is on what Joseph Ratzinger calls the 'true council' as opposed to all the 'council mischief'; this 'true council' does not denote a new beginning but simply stands in continuity with the past. The undeniably conservative passages in the council documents which the Curia forced on it are here interpreted in a decidedly backward-looking way, and the revolutionary new beginnings which point forward are passed over in decisive places.

Many people rightly speak of a betrayal of the council, a betrayal which has alienated countless Catholics from the church all over the world. Instead of the words of the conciliar programme, there are once more the slogans of a magisterium which is conservative and authoritarian. Instead of the *aggiornamento* in the spirit of the gospel, there is again the traditional integral 'Catholic teaching' (rigorous moral encyclicals, the traditionalist 'world catechism'). Instead of the 'collegiality' of the pope with the bishops, there is again a tighter Roman centralism which, in the nomination of bishops and appointments to theological chairs, sets itself above the interests of the local churches. Instead of 'openness' to the modern world, there is increasingly accusation, complaint and lamentation over alleged 'assimilation' and an encouragement of traditional forms of piety, such as Mariolatory. Instead of 'dialogue', there is again reinforced Inquisition and a refusal of freedom of conscience and teaching in the church. Instead of 'ecumenism', the emphasis is again on everything that is narrowly Roman Catholic. There is no longer any talk, as at the council, of the distinction between the church of Christ and the Roman Catholic Church, between the substance of the doctrine of faith and its garb in language and history; of a 'hierarchy of truths' which are not all equal in importance.

Even the most modest requests within Catholicism and the ecumenical world made, say, by the German, Austrian and Swiss synods – who had been working for years with much idealism, and at great cost in time, paper and finance – have been turned down or left undecided, with no reason, by a high-handed Curia. This has been accepted; who still bothers? In many places, in matters of sexual morality, mixed marriages and ecumenism, pastors and the faithful quietly do what seems right to them in the spirit of the gospel and in accordance with the impulses of Vatican II. They are not bothered about pope and bishops.

Meanwhile the Roman legalism, clericalism and triumphalism which was so vigorously criticized by the bishops at the council has come back with a vengeance – cosmetically rejuvenated and in modern dress. This became evident above all in the 'new' canon law (*Codex Iuris Canonici*) promulgated in 1983, which contrary to the intentions of the council, set virtually no limit to the exercise of power by pope, Curia and nuncios. Indeed, it diminishes the status of the ecumenical councils, assigns the conferences of bishops only advisory tasks, continues to keep the laity totally dependent on the hierarchy, and thoroughly neglects the church's ecumenical dimension.

This church 'law' is a unique instrument of power, above all for personal top decisions in the church (e.g., the nomination of cardinals which will predetermine the future papal election). Moreover, during the frequent absences of the pope it is turned into utterly practical church politics by his Curia. A wealth of new documents, ordinances, admonitions and instructions have left the Vatican: from decrees about heaven and earth to the highly ideological repudiation of the ordination of women; from the prohibition of lay preaching (even for pastoral workers with a theological training) to the prohibition of female servers at the altar; from direct interventions by the Curia in the great orders (the Jesuits, the women Carmelites, the visitation of the American congregations of sisters) to the notorious disciplinary proceedings against theologians. This pope has waged an almost spooky battle against modern women who seek a contemporary form of life, prohibiting birth control and abortion (even in the case of incest or rape), divorce, the ordination of women and the modernization of women's religious orders. Hence countless women have tacitly turned their backs on the Catholic Church, which no longer understands them. And the socialization of the young through the church largely fails to happen.

At the time of the Second Vatican Council it would hardly have been thought possible: the Inquisition is again running at full speed, especially against North American moral theologians, Central European dogmatic theologians, Latin American and African liberation theologians and Asian representatives of inter-religious dialogue. But the Jesuits, who since the council have been too progressive, are no longer in favour with Pope Wojtyla. By contrast, with every possible means he has encouraged the reactionary secret political and theological organization from Franco's Spain, Opus Dei, which has been involved in scandals connected with banks, universities and governments. The organization likewise has features characteristic of the Middle Ages and Counter-Reformation and this pope, who had close associations with it in Krakow, has withdrawn it from episcopal supervision and 'beatified' its by no means very 'holy' founder.

There has been much discussion in the media of the cost and usefulness of papal visits, though the positive aspect of them for certain nations, like the communist Poles, certainly cannot be questioned. Some spiritual impulses will have come from the numerous speeches, appeals and services. But for the church as a whole? In so many countries, have not the pope's journeys raised high hopes that something will really happen, which have then been bitterly disappointed? Often polarizations and antagonisms between those who look forward, in the perspective of the council, and traditionalists in the church are reinforced and hardened rather than being overcome. After all, this Pope not only does not heal the wounds of the church but puts salt on them, thus often encouraging more discord than harmony.

As for his own homeland of Poland, the pope is in a really tragic situation. He is the one who wanted to bring the allegedly intact anti-modern Polish Catholic model of the church to the allegedly decadent Western world, but he has had to look on impotently while the world moves in the opposite direction. Modernity is taking hold of Poland just as much as it has taken hold of Catholic Spain or Ireland. Regardless of the pope, Western secularization, individualization and pluralism are spreading everywhere. This is not necessarily negative, nor is it to be lamented in a criticism of culture.

So the chain of papal contradictions is never-ending. There is eloquent talk of human rights, but no justice is practised towards theologians and religious orders of women. There are vigorous protests against discrimination in society but discrimination is practised within the church against women, in particular in matters of birth control, abortion and ordination. There is a long encyclical on mercy, but no mercy is shown over the remarriage of divorced persons and the ten thousand married priests. And so on. In another respect, too, these are lean years. Many people are asking: What use is all the social talk about humanity, justice, peace, if the church fails above all in those social and political problems where it could itself make a decisive contribution? What is the use of pompous confessions of guilt if the pope excludes his predecessors, himself and 'the church' and does not follow them up with acts of repentance and reform?

This is true not least of the whole ecumenical sphere. No real ecumenical progress has been achieved at a single point under this pontificate – apart from the problematical Roman-Lutheran agreement on the justification of the sinner (Augsburg, 1999). On the contrary, non-Catholics speak of Roman Catholic propaganda campaigns by the pope, because their representatives are in practice welcome only as 'extras' and not as partners on an equal footing. Many indigenous Orthodox churches regard the activity of the Roman Catholic Church in the countries of Eastern Europe with a traditionally Orthodox stamp as proselytism, and this has led to tensions in the relationship between Orthodoxy and Rome. All this has resulted in an extremely disturbing cooling of the ecumenical climate, disappointment and frustration among those who are ecumenically inclined in all the churches, and also, regrettably, in a revival of the old anti-Catholic complexes and antipathies which disappeared in the 'seven fat years'.

So stagflation – stagnation of real changes and inflation of vague words and gestures – within Catholicism and stagflation in the ecumenical world meet. If John XXIII was the most significant pope of the twentieth century, John Paul II is the most contradictory.

New departures at the grass roots

However, happily the conciliar and ecumenical movement, although constantly hindered from above, continues to flourish at the grass roots, in the individual communities. The consequence is a growing alienation of the 'church from below' from the 'church from above' which goes as far as indifference. For, more than ever, how far a community is pastorally alive, liturgically active, ecumenically sensitive and socially committed depends on individual pastors and individual leading laity.

But between Rome and the communities stand the bishops, and they are very important in this crisis. At the moment the bishops – who, in many countries on all continents, are considerably more open to the needs and hopes of people than many members of the Curia at headquarters – are under a twofold pressure: from expectations at the grass roots and orders from Rome. Here the pope occasionally also uses the bishops quite personally, so that they make stands in public against the ordination of women, birth control or the counselling of women where there is a conflict of interests as to whether or not to terminate pregnancies. Personal politics is of decisive importance for longer-term changes in the Vatican, as for any other political system. And given the present Roman shift in politics, the privilege of nominating bishops (which has been increasingly appropriated by the Curia in the course of history) is beyond doubt the main instrument of oppression – if we leave aside the nominations of cardinals and the encouragement of theologians who conform with the system, both of which are the pope's sole prerogative.

More than ever it is the worldwide strategy of the Vatican successively to replace the open episcopate of the time of the council with doctrinaire bishops who fall in line, who are no less thoroughly tested for full orthodoxy, and again sworn to it, than high officials in the Kremlin used to be. But not only in the great orders of the Jesuits, Dominicans and Franciscans do people have reservations about the authoritarian pope; even in the Roman Curia there is lament and mockery at his 'Slavophilia' and the 'Polonization' of the church. Indeed the Roman Jesuit journal *Civiltà Cattolica*, in 1869/1870 a champion of the definition of infallibility, has now openly criticized in a leading article 'the excesses of the divinization of the pope and the court Byzantinism', that 'infallibilism' which is not free from 'servility' and is 'typical of a court mentality' (2 November 1985).

I sadly have to note that an unprecedented process of the

erosion of church authority is under way in many countries, accompanied by departures from the church and a largely indifferent, indeed hostile attitude towards the church in the media and the population generally. Even in the Catholic population of Germany the infallibility of the pope has lost credibility except among a small fundamentalist minority. According to a survey, only 11 per cent of Germans still regard the pope as infallible and 76 per cent support the Church and People petition (Forsa Institute, 1995) which called for change. A greater threat is that in the forty years since the council the number of regular churchgoers, young people involved in the church and church marriages, has declined by two-thirds and baptisms by one-half, whereas the numbers of candidates for the priesthood and new priests have sunk to a historic low. Soon half the posts of pastors will not be occupied. For all the influence of secularization, history will make the popes and the present Catholic bishops of Germany as responsible for this as were their predecessors in the time of the Reformation.

Behind all the current tensions, factions and confrontations are not only different persons, nations and theologies but also two different models of the church, two different 'overall constellations' or 'paradigms'. The choice is either to go back to the Roman, medieval, anti-Reformation, anti-modernist constellation, or to go forward into a modern/postmodern paradigm. So how will things develop?

There are signs of hope that the renewal of the Catholic Church is continuing, and my account of most recent church history must not be understood as pessimism or fatalism. On the contrary, the following developments have given me and others courage to go on.

1. The resistance of Catholics, men and women, to the papal policy of restoration even in traditional Catholic countries. The

results of a survey from the USA (Gallup, 1992) may be typical of most industrial countries. Of American Catholics, 87 per cent are in favour of a free decision on birth control, 75 per cent are in favour of married priests, 67 per cent are in favour of the ordination of women, 72 per cent are in favour of the election of bishops by the priest and people of the diocese, 83 per cent are in favour of condoms as a precaution against AIDS, 74 per cent are in favour of the admission to communion of divorced persons who have remarried and 85 per cent are in favour of the legalization of abortion, at least in certain circumstances; 81 per cent believe that one can be a good Catholic even if one publicly disagrees with the teaching of the church.

2. The Church and People petition in Austria (500,000 signatures) and in Germany (1,500,000 signatures) – numbers which the hierarchy has never mobilized for its position. How much commitment has been invested here by brave men and women of the now international movement 'We are the Church', which, if it is ignored by the bishops out of cowardly obedience to Rome, will yet further undermine their credibility!

3. All the active Catholic men and women all over the world at a local level: the many teachers of religion who give good lessons; the many pastors and chaplains who arrange compelling worship; the pastoral and community workers who are concerned to revive the communities; all those who work in kindergartens, hospitals and old people's homes and live out a loving Christianity; all the young people who indefatigably engage in social and ecumenical work. They all give us courage. The cause of the church is alive because it is a living one: Jesus, whom Christians for two thousand years have called the Christ.

A Vatican III with John XXIV?

That raises even more urgently the question as to how things will develop in this church and in the wider Christian world. Of course no one knows the answer, not even John Paul II, who naturally wants a John Paul III as his successor, but does not know whether perhaps a Catholic Gorbachev may be hidden among the cardinals. Even in the college of cardinals, quite a few are convinced that things cannot go on like this. If the (Roman) Catholic Church is to have a future as an institution in the twenty-first century, it needs a John XXIV. Like his predecessor in the middle of the twentieth century, he should convene a Third Vatican Council, which will lead this church from Roman Catholicism to an authentic Catholicity.

The view of the papacy held by the Catholic Church fellowship, grounded in the New Testament, is different from that of the Roman Church bureaucracy. It is the view of a pope who is not *over* the church and the world in place of God, but *in* the church as a member (instead of the head) of the people of God. It is the view of a pope who is sole ruler, but incorporated into the college of bishops, a pope who is not lord of the church but, in succession to Peter, a 'servant of the servants of God' (as Gregory the Great put it). It needed a pope like John XXIII to bring out this original view of the church and the Bishop of Rome.

For the future, this means that the problem of the Roman primacy which splits West and East so deeply must at long last be discussed openly and taken towards an ecumenical solution on the basis of the seven ecumenical councils accepted by both sides and the consensus of the early church fathers. The unhappy decisions of the First and Second Vatican Councils, made without the churches of the East, must be thought through again theologically. In the light of the extremely human figure of Peter in the New Testament and the demands of the present day, the church as a whole certainly needs more than a primacy of honour, which is ineffective in practice; it also needs more than a primacy in law, which in practice is counter-productive. It needs a constructive primacy of pastoral care, a pastoral primacy in the sense of spiritual leadership, inspiration, co-ordination and mediation – on the model of John XXIII. Is there a chance of this, perhaps after the next conclave or the next conclave but one?

In many places the spiritual and organizational vitality of the Catholic Church is unbroken; indeed, it has revived. People at the grass roots of their societies are working in solidarity with those who are suffering, with great dedication, 'on the road to Jericho': these are the 'light of the world' and 'salt of the earth'. Latin American liberation theology, Catholic peace movements in the USA and Europe, ashram movements in India and base groups in many countries in the northern and southern hemispheres are examples of how the catholicity of the Catholic Church is not just a principle of faith but a human reality which is lived out in practice.

There is nothing in the present which encourages us to hold on to illusions: resignation, frustration, indeed erosion in the fellowship of believers have left their mark on recent decades. Many people are more depressed than confident when they think of the future of the Catholic Church. But those who, like me, have experienced the historic change from Pius XII to John XXIII, which was hardly thought possible, or likewise have experienced the collapse of the Soviet empire, can say almost with confidence that a change, indeed a radical revolution, *has* to come, given the present accumulation of problems. In fact, it is only a matter of time.

Conclusion: Which Church has a Future?

Four conditions need to be met if the church is to have a future in the third millennium.

1. It must not turn backwards and fall in love with the Middle Ages or the time of the Reformation or the Enlightenment, but be a church rooted in its Christian origin and concentrated on its present tasks.

2. It must not be patriarchal, fixated on stereotyped images of women, exclusively male language and predetermined gender roles, but be a church of partnership, which combines office and charisma and accepts women in all church ministries.

3. It must not be narrowly confessional and succumb to confessional exclusiveness, the presumption of officialdom and the refusal of communion, but be an ecumenically open church, which practises ecumenism inwardly and finally follows up many ecumenical statements with ecumenical actions like the recognition of ministries, the abolition of all excommunications and complete eucharistic fellowship.

4. It must not be Eurocentric and put forward any exclusivist Christian claims and show a Roman imperialism, but be a tolerant, universal church which has a respect for the truth that is always greater; it must therefore attempt to learn from the other religions and grant an appropriate autonomy to the national, regional and local churches.

The overturning of Communism in 1989 has made it clear that the world has entered a new post-modern period: after 1918 and 1945, there is a third opportunity for a new world order which is more peaceful and more just. Will it be possible to achieve a breakthrough to a new, responsible economy which goes beyond the welfare state that we cannot afford and an antisocial neo-liberalism? And can there also be a new politics of responsibility beyond immoral *realpolitik* and immoral *idealpolitik*? Here too the demand is made to churches and religions: no peace among the nations without peace among the religions. And quite specifically the great Catholic Church is called on to fulfil urgently the four conditions mentioned above, if it is to be adequate for a new age of the world.

However, the question 'Where is the Catholic Church going?' will be misunderstood as being exclusively the church's concern unless, at the same time, thought is given to the more comprehensive problem: 'Where is humankind going?' Here, for me personally, the way is not, say, 'from the global church to a global ethic', but 'with the world church to a global ethic'. It is the search for a common ethic for humankind which can be supported by all churches and religions, indeed also by non-believers. Our globe cannot survive without a global ethic, a world ethic.

So the Catholic Church should support:

–a social world order: a society in which human beings have equal rights, live in solidarity with one another, and in which the ever-widening gulf between rich and poor is bridged;

–a plural world order: a reconciled diversity of cultures, traditions and peoples in Europe, in which there is no place for anti-Semitism and xenophobia;

–a world order in partnership: a renewed fellowship of men and women in the church and society, in which at every level women bear the same responsibility as men, and in which they can freely contribute their gifts, insights, values and experiences;

– a world order which furthers peace: a society in which the establishment of peace and the peaceful resolution of conflicts is supported, and a community of peoples who contribute in solidarity towards the well-being of others;

– a world order which is friendly to nature: a fellowship of human beings with all creatures, in which their rights and integrity are also observed;

– an ecumenical world order: a community that creates the presuppositions for a peace among the nations through a unity of confessions and peace among the religions.

It is impossible for me to predict when and how this vision of a Catholic Church renewed in accordance with the gospel of Jesus Christ will be realized. But throughout my life as a theologian I have indefatigably written that this vision can become reality and shown how that can happen. Despite the present ecumenical 'low', I have the well-founded hope that Christianity will finally find its way to an ecumenical paradigm in the present upheaval between modernity and post-modernity. For the new generation, the time of confessionalism is finally in the past. Granted, the traces of the 'confessional paradigms' will continue to be evident. A uniform Christianity is neither probable nor desirable. But after the abolition of all reciprocal excommunications, the confessions will be abolished and transcended by a new communication, indeed an ecumenical communion – this primarily means eucharistic fellowship, but also the fellowship of Christians in everyday life.

Such an ecumenical paradigm will no longer be characterized by three antagonistic confessions, but only by three complementary basic attitudes. This means three questions will be asked and answered in this way:

• Who is orthodox? Those who are particularly concerned with 'right teaching', true teaching, are orthodox. To be specific, they are concerned with that truth which, because it is God's truth, cannot be given to the individual (Christians, bishops, churches) at random, but rather is to be handed down creatively to ever new generations, and lived out by the faithful tradition of the whole church. Now if this is decisively 'orthodox', then it is the case that an evangelical or a catholic Christian too can, and must, be orthodox in this sense, of 'true teaching'.

• Who is catholic? Those who are particularly concerned with the whole, universal, comprehensive church are catholic. To be specific: it is those who are interested in the continuity and universality of faith and the community of faith in time and space despite all the breaks. Now if this is what is decisively 'catholic', an orthodox or an evangelical Christian too can, and must, be catholic in this sense, of universal breadth.

• Finally, who is evangelical? Those who are particularly concerned constantly to refer to the gospel in all church traditions, teachings and practices. To be specific: it is those who reflect on Holy Scripture and on constant practical reform according to the norm of the gospel. And if this is what is decisively 'evangelical', then finally it is the case that orthodox and catholic Christians too can, and must, be evangelical in this sense, being inspired by the gospel.

Rightly understood, even today 'orthodox', 'catholic' and 'evangelical' basic attitudes are no longer exclusive but complementary. And this is not just a postulate but a fact: all over the world, even now countless Christians, communities and groups are in practice living out an authentic ecumenicity centred on the gospel – despite all the resistance in the church structures. It is a great and important task for the future to convince more and more Catholics of this.

Chronological table

185–251   Origen
249–51   First general persecution of Christians under the Emperor
          Decius

III   THE IMPERIAL CATHOLIC CHURCH

313   The Emperor Constantine guarantees freedom of religion
325   The Emperor Constantine sole ruler
          First Council of Nicaea
354–430   Aurelius Augustine (from 395 Bishop of Hippo)
381   First Council of Constantinople
          The Emperor Theodosius the Great declares Catholic
          doctrine the state religion and later prohibits all pagan
          cults
395   Death of Theodosius and division of the Roman empire
          into an Eastern and a Western empire
410   Conquest of 'Eternal Rome', by Alaric's West Goths
431   Council of Ephesus

IV   THE PAPAL CHURCH

440–61   Pope Leo the Great
451   Council of Chalcedon
476   Downfall of the West Roman empire
492–6   Pope Gelasius I
498/499   Baptism of Clovis, king of the Franks
527–65   Emperor Justinian
553   Second Council of Constantinople
590–604   Pope Gregory the Great
622   Beginning of the Islamic era
681   Third Council of Constantinople
787   Second Council of Nicaea
800   Coronation of Charlemagne in St Peter's
858–67   Pope Nicholas I
1046   Synods of Sutri and Rome with the deposition of three
          rival popes by King Henry III

V THE CHURCH IS SPLIT

VI REFORM, REFORMATION OR COUNTER-REFORMATION?

1950   Dogma of Mary's physical assumption into heaven.
Encyclical *Humani generis* against the errors of the time
1958–63   Pope John XXIII: encyclical *Pacem in terris*
1962–5   Second Vatican Council
1963–78   Pope Paul Paul VI
1967   Encyclical *Sacerdotalis coelibatus* for compulsory celibacy
1968   Encyclical *Humanae vitae* against contraception
1978   Pope John Paul I
1978   Pope John Paul II

Index